THE NEW TRACTATUS

Summing Up Everything

Bruce Fleming

University Press of America,® Inc.
Lanham · Boulder · New York · Toronto · Plymouth, UK

University Press of America,® Inc.
4501 Forbes Boulevard
Suite 200
Lanham, Maryland 20706
UPA Acquisitions Department (301) 459-3366

Estover Road
Plymouth PL6 7PY
United Kingdom

Library of Congress Control Number: 2007930026
ISBN-13: 978-0-7618-3796-1 (paperback : alk. paper)
ISBN-10: 0-7618-3796-5 (paperback : alk. paper)

♾™ The paper used in this publication meets the minimum
requirements of American National Standard for Information
Sciences—Permanence of Paper for Printed Library Materials,
ANSI Z39.48—1984

Table of Contents

Preface

*Like Ludwig Wittgenstein, I believe that big topics can be covered in little ground. In his **Tractatus Logico-Philosophicus**, Wittgenstein offered what he thought was a philosophy to end all philosophy, ordered in seven propositions with sub-propositions. Every new whole number, 1, 2, and so on up to 7, is a new major topic. 1.1 is a sub-topic to 1.0, 1.11 of 1.1 (and so on).*

*This is the **New Tractatus**: informed by what I take to be the essential spirit of the "old" one, but making this essential spirit clearer than it was in Wittgenstein's work, then reacting to it and taking it in a different direction. The **New Tractatus** uses the same numbering system as the old, though I've begun with a 0.0 proposition as a preamble and have used the seventh proposition to its full length.*

Wittgenstein was concerned with questions like how language could mean anything, what our relationship to the universe is, and the nature of philosophy itself. I treat these, and many other topics, such as: Why is sex such a hot potato? Why are we so interested in celebrities? What is the nature of love? Why do liberals and conservatives argue about so many things? What is magic? Can miracles happen? Is science objective? Does art lie to us? How do we win arguments? What is the meaning of life? It's not technical philosophy, any more than these are technical topics. People can read it on the train, on the beach, or in the carrel of a library.

*The **New Tractatus** shares with the old the fundamental perception that we can never transcend what is. On the cover of a guide book to Mexico I found this: "Wherever you go, there you are!" You achieve the foreign, and find the domestic. Before you got there it was foreign because you weren't there; after you're there it's once again the taste of your own saliva and the grittiness of sand under your feet. And you have to find a new "foreign." You never eliminate things beyond you in the world, you just change your relationship to them. But that changes the things themselves. The universe works, in philosophical terms, on a conservation of matter basis: nothing is ever created or destroyed, just rearranged. We're the ones rearranging it.*

Thus order can be created in the world, but it isn't created in absolute terms. Order in the world is silhouetted against the disorder that this action hasn't affected, and the "waste" disorder that the act of focusing on this order has produced: while we're doing this, we're failing to do many other things, which probably go even further to seed than they would have done. Our world is all of this: the creation of order, the disorder this action itself adds to, and the action that takes us between these realms. At any one time, we're in one part of this cycle, but that means that at the same time, we're working out the whole cycle.

The whole of Wittgenstein's **Tractatus** is summed up in its opening phrase: "Die Welt ist alles, Was der Fall ist." The standard translation of Pears and McGuinness rendered this as a statement about statements: "The world is everything that is the case." This translation helped ensure that Wittgenstein's **Tractatus** was initially read as an essay on language. This led to the Vienna School of logical positivism, exemplified by Carnap, whose mission was to purify language of the things that were getting in the way of perfect picturing of facts. What a bizarre fate for a book about the ineffability of language!

The **Tractatus** is more profoundly seen as being about the strange fact that whatever you've said, you've said it, so it too is part of the world. Even what you'd like to take out, or pretend doesn't exist—say, mistakes—still did happen, and all this too is part of the world. Life is the whole transcript, not the edited version. This is what Wittgenstein meant, I believe, when he said, in 5.473, "We cannot, in a certain sense, make mistakes in logic." They're part of reality too. We see another version of this same idea in 2.063: "The sum-total of reality is the world."("Die gesamte Wirklichkeit ist die Welt"; here the standard translation seems more to the point.)

I express this idea that everything is part of life—not just the motion forward we put on our resumé—as "living in error"—as in NT 1.1. "Life consists of realizing what we didn't know before. This means that most of life consists of living in error." Or NT 1.11: "Life consists of learning things." We emphasize the result, perhaps even denying what it took to achieve that result: but this emphasis hasn't made the motion toward the result disappear, and life is thus both the time before and the achieved result—as well as the time after.

It makes more sense to translate the opening of the **Tractatus** as follows: "The world is everything that is."("Der Fall" in German can also mean an instance of something, "the case of x"—something real, not used merely in the abstract sense of "being the case," where in this phrase we don't know what "the case" is.) Or just as likely: "Everything that is: that constitutes the world." It's similar to 2.063, "The sum-total of reality is the world." This gives us a sense of the shoulder-shrugging "that's the way it is" quotidian nature of life that is at the center of Wittgenstein's **Tractatus**. We can apparently escape what we have, but whatever we get is then also what we have.

Many individual propositions of the **New Tractatus** *could serve as a comparably efficient sum-up of this work, in the way that the opening of the* **Tractatus** *can for it. One is this: NT 1.811 "The feeling of control and predictability is always based on things we have under control, not on the things we fail to have under control." Or this: NT 7.6 "We spend our lives in the attempt to pin things down, make the world certain. In the moment of pinning down, it feels as if we have achieved our goal. But we have only pinned down one thing, the thing we are considering right here, right now." We don't create more of anything in the world, just re-arrange what's here already.*

The painter Ferdinand Léger was mesmerized by the beauty of machine-like shapes, the gizmos of industrialization. So, to a degree, was Wittgenstein, in his case things like truth tables and mathematical formulae. Thus it's not merely Wittgenstein's readers, but Wittgenstein himself who overplayed his fascination with a vision of a crystalline world: the utterances themselves were lapidary, and all those truth tables seemed so nicely objective—in the service, paradoxically, of a philosophy of what couldn't be said. Perhaps Wittgenstein was merely falling prey to the lure that the machine-like has for the young, while simultaneously realizing its insufficiency.

Still, it seems Wittgenstein did think that he could talk people into silence. The **New Tractatus,** *by contrast, is imbued with the fatalism—and thus perhaps realism—of the not-quite-so-young. I say, with a shrug: All you're doing is changing the position of things. But sure. Go ahead—talk away. eople will anyway, since each new person, each new generation, has to have a swing at the paradoxes of the human condition—such as, among others, this one: that transcendence is always a response to and within the context of the non-transcendent—and each attempt to cut off the head of the Hydra of talk, each attempt to get everybody to Solve the Big Problems once and for all, merely causes more heads to sprout, more talk to flow.*

Why wouldn't it? Other people have to live too, and that means: others have to do things their own way. Each person has to mature, and find love, and decide what the universe is up to. It seems crabbed and strange to think that we're going to do this so well that they needn't, as if we thought a man could shave so well today he wouldn't ever have to do it tomorrow. That's only true if there is no tomorrow, when he dies.

The sense that Wittgenstein thought he was going to put muzzles on people who didn't say what he wanted to hear is what's soured a generation or two on the **Tractatus,** *now almost universally laid aside in* *favor of the **Philosophical Investigations**. For, after a "l'entre-les-deux-guerres" infatuation with the **Tractatus** came the recoil: the picture theory was wrong! Now, of course, we know that "meaning is use."*

*But "early" and "late" Wittgenstein (as we sometimes call the identical author of these two respective works) merely offer two different emphases within the same world-view. Either we emphasize that we can get somewhere else than where we are now, achieve the exotic, or we point out that we don't achieve it for very long, and have to move on. Both of these positions are part of the world, and that's what Wittgenstein seemed to have been aiming at in the **Tractatus**. You can't get beyond what is. Both the going and the moving on are part of the world. Wherever you go, there you are!*

*Wittgenstein's famous last line in the **Tractatus** is this: "Alles, Was nicht gesagt werden kann, darüber muss man schweigen." "As for everything that can't be said: we just have to [in the sense of prediction] fall silent about that."*

Pears and McGuinness translate this as: "What we cannot speak about we must pass over in silence." As in: I have things to say but am not allowed to say them? I think it unlikely Wittgenstein meant we were capable of forming phrases that nonetheless were not permitted to exit our mouths or flow from our pens. It's too inconsistent with his sense that people are going to do what they do, that whatever we do, that's part of the world too. ("The sum-total of reality is the world.") I think he meant that once you'd articulated both the transcendence and the fact that it was a reaction to the non-transcendent, you'd just have to shrug your shoulders. If he really meant to forbid something he could have done it this way: "Alles, Was nicht gesagt werden kann, darf nicht gesagt werden." "Everything that can't be said: that may not be said." Or perhaps this: "Alles, Was nicht gesagt werden kann, das soll man nicht sagen." "We shouldn't speak what can't be said." But see how ridiculous we sound if we actually articulate the meaning so many have thought these phrases to have. Why shouldn't we say these things? Who's stopping us?

In fact, this last line reads to me like a shrug: "Everything that can't be said— you just have to fall silent about that." Not "be silent," as in: don't even try to articulate the both/and of two alternatives one of which denies the other. Instead: Sure, try, go ahead. But in the end, he knows we'll just give up. It's not so much an order as a prediction. We can't order two contraries into anything larger. We take them one at a time, in alternation.

The American transcendentalist Margaret Fuller is said to have announced, grandeloquently: "I accept the universe!" When someone repeated this to Thomas Carlyle, he's supposed to have responded: "Egad! She'd better."

I share Carlyle's bemusement at such grand pronouncements by individuals. The universe doesn't care whether we accept it or not. Still, we might as well accept it. Once you realize that all of this is life—not just the moment you succeed in jumping off the ground, but the preparation for the jump, the jump, the descent, and finding yourself back on solid ground—why not accept the fact with enthusiasm as well as with resignation?

Arguments arise between people about issues for the same reason they arose between the blind men each of whom had his hands on a specific part of the elephant. The man touching the leg announced that the elephant "was very like a tree!"; the man with his hand on the trunk that it was "very like a snake." We try to equate all of life with a fragment, getting the other blind men who assert that the elephant is too like a snake or a tree to see things our way. Sure, we can try. And probably we're condemned to, given that we're all in the position of the blind men. But we never transcend the position of the blind men. Offering an over-view that includes the points of view of the other blind men is something a single blind man can do. But this doesn't end the argument. It just takes its place in the flow, especially as there's no guarantee the other blind men will be interested in such an over-view, at least not then.

*If Wittgenstein did believe he could talk himself, or others, into silence, he found out he was wrong by living on after the **Tractatus** and responding to its reception. Philosophy begets philosophy; a response begets another response. In everyday terms, this means that the next person is going to have to have his or her say, whatever we think we've done. We don't stop time or make anything definitive by wrapping it up and putting a bow on it. The next person refuses the package, or opens it and uses the contents for something else entirely.*

*Wittgenstein said he thought his **Tractatus** could only be understood by someone who had thought the same things. I think pretty nearly everybody has thought about the things covered in the **New Tractatus**.*

Annapolis, Maryland
1 May 2007

Dem Andenken meines Bruders Keith,
und allen AIDS-Opfern, gewidmet

What's the point of asking questions?

0 Because we're alive, we're creatures of motion, and so, creatures of change. Our lowest level of activity is not motionlessness, even if we think we're sitting still.

0.1 The default position of life is like a moving stream on which we drift.

We can swim faster than the current, sideways, or even against it. But doing what seems to us "nothing" is not, in absolute terms, nothing: we're still in motion, like a car whose neutral gear is set to run at a mile or two an hour.

0.11 We're not responsible for making the current go forwards.

We didn't invent the world that allows us to invent things.

0.2 At any given time we're concerned with a small number of things. Usually we're concerned with one thing. And then another, and then another.

0.3 Being concerned with one thing means we fail to be concerned with all the others.

For us they don't exist, until we have reason to be concerned with them, at which point they do.

0.31 All things we're concerned with are finite.

0.32 The more we concentrate on a single thing, the more absolutely all the others disappear from our concentration. We may not even understand why everyone else is not concentrating on the same thing we are. It seems so self-evident to do so.

0.33 We're likely to try to make other people be concerned with what concerns us. This may be so for the best of motives: this subject seems of overwhelming importance, say being saved in an afterlife, or eradicating world poverty, or not drinking alcohol, or supporting the X political party.

0.331 Those people intensely concerned with a certain question or problem will insist that the world will end if others don't consider this question or problem too. But this is merely the way it seems to them. It may not seem so to others. The failure to consider any particular question or issue is merely a failure to consider that issue, as considering that issue is a failure to consider all others.

We need not let ourselves be bullied by the intrinsic limitation of human attention.

0.4 All the things we consider are moved up one by one from the vast storage house of the unconsidered. We cannot define the storage house itself, because this too is a specific idea we are considering, and so part of the contents of the storage house.

Perhaps there is no storage house.

0.5 Fundamental stands in inverse relation to useful. Consider the claim that we must, willy nilly, be following moral rules A, B, and C, or that the structure of thought is D, E, and F. If things are so fundamental as to be inescapable, then even denying them doesn't affect them (this was the ingenious realization of Marx and Freud).[1]

So what do they matter? (Marx and Freud thought this meant they mattered more than anything else). Fundamental turns out to be a quality in inverse relationship to useful.

0.51 Saying that a specific structure or idea is more fundamental than others is thinking like Dr. Seuss's Yertle the Turtle.[2] Yertle stood on a stack of turtles and proclaimed himself king of all he could see. By this definition he was the king of a far-off house, a tree, and a mule—and, as the stack of conscripted turtles under him grew and he was raised so high he could see further, of even more. Yet what he doesn't consider is that the tree was unaware of being under the sovereignty of Yertle. Fundamental Structures and Principles are like that too: I, the Most Fundamental X, control you, and you, and you! What if you are unaware of being controlled? What if you deny it? The tree was unaware of being under Yertle's suzerainty, and so continued as it was.

0.52 The more contenders there are for Most Fundamental Idea or Most Basic Structure—and there will certainly be more than one as people realize the apparent advantage of the position—the sooner we are likely to roll our eyes. Take a number, we'll say. The world is full of Most Fundamentals.

0.53 These at least are contenders for the same thing, and so are in opposition. Most of the things in the world are not in opposition to the rest. They are simply unrelated.

0.531 The articles about books in a single issue of, say, *The New York Review of Books* typically cluster several books on the same theme: say, the French Revolution, or global warming. [3] This leads us to think the world is in order. These two or three books cover the same ground, perhaps even agree or disagree with each other. But think of the dizzying dips and dives of subject matter in the books reviewed in any one issue of the periodical. What has the life of Poet X to do with Middle Eastern politics or with a new theory of evolution or with an explanation of how the mind works or with fifteenth-century warfare? None of the people considered in these is paying the slightest attention to the others. Nor are the authors of the books necessarily reading the other books.

0.5311 Hemingway tells us that Gertrude Stein and James Joyce, both living in Paris in the 20s and both influential Modernists, made sure never to meet.[4] If someone made the mistake of mentioning Joyce to Gertrude Stein, he was never invited back to 27, rue de Fleurus. Gertrude Stein didn't need Joyce. She had Alice—and Basket, her poodle. "I am I if my little dog knows me," she said.[5]

0.532 Things that conflict are the tiniest tips of icebergs on the vast mass of things that have nothing to do with one another.

0.54 We focus on the conflicts because they are more exciting than a lack of conflict. Conflicts beg to be resolved. Yet the paradox is, positions even more divergent than these in conflict are so divergent they don't conflict. And these vastly outnumber the conflicts. A law of physics may be more fundamental than any particular moving bodies that exhibit it, but how does it relate to (say) a sense of humor? What have breezes to do with botulism, or with books? Or any of these to do with potty-training my two-year-old?

0.54 Some people have thought the most absolute dichotomy we can name is the dichotomy between the mind and the body. This odd notion came from thinking that everything in the body's world could be put in relation to everything else, say in the grid of time and space, and nothing in the mind's world could be put in relation to anything: in the mind things drift.

But it's not true that everything in the world is related to everything else. We only come to believe this because we make the largest possible sketch of the world, and don't fill it in. We make a map of the largest land bodies: there, see? We've mapped the world.

This gives us an unjustified sense of control of the body's world, which makes us think it different from the world of the mind.

Nor is it true that the things in the mind are more unrelated than any other things. Let's say suddenly we remember a long-gone relative. We don't know why: we just did. The map of the mind seems imprecise. But by the same token, do we know why the napkin crumpled just this way, the water splattered into this pattern, or my right index finger just as long as it is? At best we can offer the explanations we have developed why paper crumples, water splatters, and fingers are within a scale of normal. We've drawn the biggest outlines so it seems to us the world is covered. And sometimes we do have resons why we thought of Great Uncle Joe: we just saw someone who looks like him. Or: it's Christmas, his favorite holiday.

To the extent that we make the same sketches of the world of the mind, we may begin to think that "covered" too.

It won't be any more covered than the world of the body is.

0.6 What we concentrate on in the world—what gives us the sense that the world, unlike the mind, is solid—is a pearl in a string, to which will at some point (a moment later? next year? in a book by someone not yet born?) be added another pearl, and another, and another. We search through a vast table of pearls for just the one that fits. What we focus on is the one that fits, not the thousands that don't.

0.7 At some point we die, which breaks our concentration on whatever topic we were concentrating on. It turns out not to be true that we absolutely positively had to solve this problem.

0.71 Everything we do is part of the pattern of our life, whether this consists of creating a structure, rebelling against the structure, denying the structure, or propping it up. Whether we are shrieking in frustration or humming in pleasure, all this is part of the history of who we are.

0.8 The boats held up by the water don't need to know how deep the water is, so long as it is holding them up. It only matters if they get close to rocks or land.

So long as the boat floats, we don't have to plumb the depths. The only thing that matters is that the keel clears.

Being held up is the default of life. Difficulties are always particular, and require particular reactions.

0.81 Any peering over the boat's side into the depths is for a specific reason: this action by itself is always logically subsequent to the fact that the water holds up the boat. We don't have to know how deep the water is to confirm that the boat floats.

The primordial state is of the boat floating. Any difficulties are subsequent. We can deal with them, but as they arise.

0.82 We can try to predict difficulties that have yet to arise, but even these are specific predictions, made at a specific time. Even they presuppose the boat's floating.

0.83 At death, the boat ceases to float. Death is a boundary, not an event.

0.84 Anything that happens before death is an event, not a boundary.

0.9 Whatever we do in our life is part of our life, the design it makes.

No particular thing we do in life can explain what allows us to do the whole thing, even if that is an explanation. The explanation is part of life.

0.91 No particular thing is essential. The proof is, we could fail to do it and this failure too would be part of our life, part of the design we make. Or the person next to us could fail to do it, and probably will. If that person did it, in fact, why should we? If it's so important, why didn't everyone before us do it already?

0.92 Life is more than the sum of its parts. Anything we say or do is one of the parts of life, never its totality.

What kind of knowledge is attainable?

1 We're all beginners at the game of life.
1.1 Life consists of realizing what we didn't know before. This means that most of life consists of living in error.

1.11 Usually we put it this way: life consists of learning things.

Several nights in a row I heard what seemed like scratching noises on the roof. The first time or two I was half asleep, and managed to ignore them. The third or fourth time, I lay awake listening to them. What were they? I didn't know. Tree branches in the wind? Not the right sound. Squirrels?

The next night, this time waiting for the noise, I lay awake until I heard the sound of something walking across the roof. Then silence, then scratching over my head. Clearly an animal. But it was still a shock to me when, the next night, armed with a flashlight, I shone the beam into the face of a raccoon, pausing long enough in its crawl up the drainpipe to look down at me indignantly.

This ended almost a week of not knowing what was causing the noise, a week that did not for that reason cease to be part of my life.

What to do? Once again, something I didn't know. Here my not knowing was measured in terms of a few days. I reasoned that probably I wasn't the first person to have this problem, or the only one in our wooded county. Clearly I could have someone take care of the problem. But what was such a person called?

A day or two went by before my mother suggested I look under "Trappers" in the yellow pages. This produced results. It turned out there were in fact trappers, unsurprisingly called "trappers," who did this sort of thing all the time.

And so, two days later there was a trap on my roof that, in short order, caught a mother raccoon and three babies. At first I assumed the animals would be released. I was wrong about this too. There was no point in mercy, the trapper explained: fully half the raccoons in our county were rabid, and in any case they had uncanny memories. If released elsewhere they would manage to find their way back to my attic.

During the time period I dealt with this problem the amount of being right was miniscule compared to the amount of being wrong. When the problem was solved, I went on to other problems. They too were situations in which I was wrong.

1.2 At any given moment the things we're wrong about or worse, ignorant of, are exponentially greater than the things we're right about.

We're constantly bumping our nose against things, and having to deal with the consequences. These show us that we were misinformed.

We're constantly taking two steps forward and one step back, or several, and then again, and then again.

1.21 Having to stop to figure things out stops the flow of things.

1.22 We only learn things when the world goes contrary to our expectations.

1.23 The impetus for figuring things out comes from outside. Most ignorance is simply unresolved, or more usually still, passes unperceived.

Virginia Woolf wrote an essay called "The Mark on the Wall" about how she didn't know what a certain blob on the wall one evening (as we would say) really *was*.[6] She could see it was a mark, but what kind of mark? Was it a nail? A smudge? She noted that the world usually demands that we hide from others the time when we're not sure about things. We're supposed to meet others with confident faces. We end up denying that we were ever unsure at all.

For Woolf, this attitude was a lie, compounded by male bravado that always asserted it knew more than it did in order to impress the competition. It seemed a constituent part of the illusion of order created in English society before the First World War, where to know whether a Bishop went in to dinner before or after a

General, one simply consulted a document known the Table of Precedency in Whittaker's Almanac, listing what seemed the absolute order of the world, from the Sovereign on down. In the post-War world in which Woolf wrote, this Table, once so firm and established, was no longer consulted. Its power was broken. It hadn't ceased to exist; instead people had merely turned away. They focused on other things that had been there all along.

Everything we're sure of is as potentially transitory as Whittaker's Table of Precedency. Only we don't know how long it will last. Potentially transitory turns out to be indistinguishable from potentially permanent. This is the paradox of the world. Knowledge too, the state of certainty, turns out to be itself built on the sands of time.

Woolf admitted she could get up and look at the mark to find what the blob was. But that, she suggested, would be to give in to the false clarity that so obscures the way life really feels: the sense of being in possession of knowledge, and one's self. Most of the time we're not composed and poised, or in control. Instead, she suggested, we're blown along by the wind with our hair flying out, the objects we've lost swirling about us.

The mark was a snail, she tells us. But we're not supposed to exhale and give a big grin when we find out. We're supposed to say: Oh. Now does that make things better?

Let's say our goal is to find out what the mark is. In this case, finding out is better than not finding out, knowing than not knowing. But for each mark discovered to be a snail there are many other things that remain unknown. And while we're finding out the mark was a snail, we're leaving unfollowed other pathways, insuring our ignorance about all these things.

1.3 Life consists of being in error regarding the people we live with as well.

1.31 This is the sign of living in error: "It seemed like a good idea at the time." That means, we now realize it wasn't.

1.32 Dating, auditioning sexual or life-partners, consists of constantly forming views of the person we are trying on for size. We ask ourselves (it may be) such questions as these: Does she have a nice smile? Is she interesting? Is she interested in me? Is she talking too much about her ex? In the early moments or hours of a date we may find ourselves revising our views a hundred times. The speed of interrogation slows down if we become involved with the person, but for that reason the alterations that inevitably do occur increase in power. Because we think we know the person we're with, we are hit that much harder when we're forced to conclude that we don't.

1.33 The main character in Tolstoy's "Kreutzer Sonata," who by the time he tells his story has killed his wife for having what he believed was an affair with a violinist, recounts his changing feelings after the first argument they had.[7] What he didn't know at the time was that it would represent the first swing of a pendulum, the first saw-tooth of a series of up-and-down arguments. After each new argument, he had to change his interpretation of what had happened. Having had a single argument implies one thing to him about their relationship, two arguments implies another, three yet another. By the fourth we must say that it is habitual behavior, which implies yet something else. We are always playing catch-up ball in our understanding of things.

This is so because understanding is understanding of something we didn't previously understand.

"The Kreutzer Sonata" is also about the fact that the husband may have been wrong about the most basic thing he takes for granted, namely that his wife was having an affair with a violinist. To be sure, the husband had come home to find the violinist dining and making music with his wife, alone, when the husband was believed to be away. But did this indicate an affair? Or was this, as his wife insisted, merely her attempt to have a friend? That seems impossible to the husband. His conclusion is that men and women do not belong together as sexual partners in marriage; they're just too different.

1.34 I see my father in one way when I am 10, another when I am 20, another by the time I am 40, and several others after that. I like my job, then don't, then do again. At each point I decide I was wrong before.

1.35 The same is true of briefer relationships. A new colleague arrives at work. I form one view of him based on what I see the first day, revise it a week later when I realize he's said something odd for the third time, then again a month later when he opens up to me at the water cooler and explains his odd behavior. Most people never open up to us at all, and who says that we will stay with this view of them we get after a month?

1.4 We are constantly learning new things about ourselves. This means the old view of ourselves was wrong.

We realize after many years we were (say) only putting on an act for someone, perhaps even ourselves, when we said we liked going to the beach. Or that the apologetic second nature we had developed was only the result of trying to please someone, a parent or a sibling, by doing X or Y. Or that the reason a marriage was such a disaster was that we didn't think ourselves worthy of true happiness. Or that, much to our surprise, we do too like sexual act A or B that initially had seemed so strange. Or food C or D. Or painter E or F. We didn't say any of these things before, because (as we say) we didn't know they were true. We could have passed a lie detector test saying they weren't true. Nonetheless we conclude they weren't.

1.41 We learn more about ourselves and other people over time.

"More" is defined with respect to what we knew before about the person we learn about, not to an absolute amount.

We shake our heads when we think of all the many things we didn't know about ourselves at 16, perhaps also at 20, or even 30. By about 30 we should have settled down a bit, be in possession of the most fundamental knowledge about ourselves. We should know that we tend to react thus and so in this kind of situation, we should know what our "type" in (say) women is. We will know what wines we prefer, and what kind of desserts. We should know whether we like to exercise, and what we like to do on vacation.

But how dearly was this knowledge bought! When we consider what we know, we don't usually consider the pains of acquiring this knowledge, and how long it took us to get it. So many things we did in our youth simply because others wanted us to do them, or because it was expected of us! And why not? We had to do them to discover we didn't want to.

1.5 We think of knowledge as money in a bank account. Things we know are so much substantial stuff. But each bit of knowledge is solid in one direction only, by contrast with not knowing it before. At its other boundary it falls off into ignorance.

A piece of music comes on the radio. I am proud of myself that I can immediately identify it as a Romantic violin sonata. I realize moreover it is the only sonata by César Franck. If I stop there I have substantiality, a good deal more than most people. (My mother was a music professor and my brother a cellist.) I know who wrote this music.

But what do I really know about Franck? Not even his birth dates. Nor what he looked like. I know he wrote a famous symphony, but I don't know about his other works, or where he was born. A music professor would presumably know these things, but even his or her knowledge would at some point sputter out. We can know more than other people, but with respect to all there is to know what we have is rather pitiful.

1.51 Ignorance and knowledge are not clearly delineated. One implies the other.

What if I say, hearing this sonata, that it's by Brahms? This is wrong. But isn't it less wrong than saying it's by Mozart? At least the general time period is correct if I say Brahms. Or if I can't name a name, I say it sounds like that one we heard, you know, that concert a year ago... Do we say I know something, or that I don't? I know something if we cut the cake from one direction, and am ignorant if we cut it in another.

1.52 Each hard gem of knowing something is the tip of an iceberg of not knowing.

We are largely unaware of this mass of ignorance because we're not forced by others to look down at it.

1.521 The once case when we are is when we adopt the learning position.

1.53 There are two positions with respect to the world, teaching and learning. When we teach others, we look away from the limits of our knowledge; when we are in the learning position we are facing, all the time and relentlessly, toward them.

Whether or not we take information on board is determined by whether or not we have assumed the learning position. If we have not assumed this position, we take nothing on board.

1.531 Our society typically puts us in the learning position in our early years, and in the teaching position in our later ones.

We say we know more as we age because most of us get jobs that allow us to repeat the small amount of things we know, and do over and over the one or two things we do better than the next person. But most of us who are competent in our narrow niche couldn't pass the simplest test in a general high school subject in other niches, even in things we once knew. We become specialists and forget the rest. And the further we are from the things we've forgotten, the more incompetent we become in them. We have the sense of knowing more simply because we are more deeply entrenched in the small part of the world we are comfortable in. We just don't come in contact with the rest.

1.532 Most people rebel against being in the learning position as they reach the time we designate as adulthood. Partly this is cause, and partly effect: adulthood is when we know people will tire of being told what to do; they tire because they see adulthood approaching.

It's not that they know everything there is to know, simply that they are tired of the learning position.

1.6 The conviction that we know more the more candles we have on our birthday cake is based only on a metaphor, just as the image of traveling down a road in life and being able to look back at the increasing distance we've traveled is an image. We speak of the "weight of the years," as if we keep adding things to ourselves as we age. Like all metaphors, this can control our thought. At the same time, we can change the words we use to express this. (Most words aren't metaphors.) [8]

What if instead we think of ourselves as comets? We travel across the sky, changing position and burning up rather than accumulating. At each moment we push into the air, and the result is our fire. Our tail may get longer, but it's just ourselves being used up. We don't accumulate wisdom, we use up our impulsion forward.

1.61 The "wisdom" of age isn't having more of something substantial, it's just having a different something than we had before. We know things from a different perspective.

1.611 Youth always thinks it knows more than old age, simply because it's simply unaware of problems it has yet to face. Things seem simple to the young. So the natural reaction of the old, seeing that things are complex, is to say, we know more.

1.612 What we know is that youth will some day be where we are now.

1.613 If we're middle-aged, we know different things than when we were young, and may even know something about the young. But we still don't yet know about old age. When we get to old age, we find that our knowledge of old age makes youth so far away we're uninterested in it, or too interested, rather than taking it for granted as the young do.

1.614 This may be what T.S. Eliot meant when he said, "There is . . . only a limited value in the knowledge derived from experience."[9]

1.7 Wisdom consists of moving to a higher level of generality with respect to what we have. The terms we use to describe what we see are more general. Learning consists of ordering the world into columns, establishing types. All of us order particulars under larger themes.

If male, we typically start out with particular females, say Sadie and add Patience and Martha, and by the time we are 40 we have a notion of "women." Yet it may not be the same view of "women" as the view of the next man. And even our view changes as we get to know Hope and Charity, and then Yvonne and Isolde. More specifics change the nature of the general.

1.71 The increased ability, with age, to "put things in perspective" implies an increasing and related inability to see the individuals with the absoluteness we once did.

1.72 In gaining access to generals, we typically become less interested in particulars. And in any case we see them differently. Another city is merely another city, not an exciting experience, another plane ride another plane ride. Even if we have an unusually good experience on the plane ride itself, this is typically accompanied by a sense of melancholy: another trip, another arrival. This sense of "same old, same old" in itself is a new experience, something the young do not (and probably should not) feel.

1.721 Sometimes men settle down with a single woman when they see the types begin to repeat. Why not this particular example of the type? they think.

1.8 We can solve particular problems in life, but we can't solve all problems, for all time. (See 0.6.)

If we get things in one portion of our life under control, we leave vast plots open to other problems. If we have left these fields fallow and untended, here is where problems will grow. Thus we are always surprised by new problems.

1.81 Only by focusing on the orderly parts and shutting out the disorderly ones can we convince ourselves we have things under control.

1.811 The feeling of control and predictability is always based on things we have under control, not on the things we fail to have under control.

We get up one morning and realize that for many years we have been deluding ourselves and simply cannot do so one day longer. Say, in thinking that we love our spouse. Or, suddenly we see our mother in a new way as we realize she has turned into a crotchety old woman. Or our son is hauled off to prison: we have to revise what we think we know. Perhaps we were spending so much time in our job we have been neglecting him? Perhaps no amount of time with him could have prevented this from happening? Suddenly these are problems. Yet apparently they were there before.

1.82 Our need to feel we are in increasingly greater control of the world tends to work against flexibility as we age. We react the way we've been taught to react, rather than the way that works best with this new circumstance.

1.83 The more firmly we fence ourselves into a world where we know things, the more certain it is that we will either be broadsided by things outside that narrow world, or make ourselves irrelevant.

1.831 Wisdom involves acknowledging the things we don't know, and that we don't even know we don't know.

Why do we want the things we want?

Projects and goals

2 Our projects are what give us goals, which in turn give us a reason for acting.

2.01 Our lives are given motion forward through projects, which can come from others, or from ourselves.

"What are you doing?" someone might ask. "I'm going to the store," I answer. Or: "I'm working on my book." Or: "I'm trying to save enough to put the kids through college." Great chunks of the day, week, month, and decade are ordered all at once through the vector arrows of our goals.

2.02 We focus on the things we learn rather than the fact that for most of the time we didn't know them because that gives us a sense of moving forward. (See 1.2). It makes us feel we are mastering our environment.

2.03 Projects become what we fulfill. They become their own ends. We complete limited structures.

We begin by putting two coins next to each oher, and make the collection of other coins our goal. We begin by amassing X dollars and make 10X our goal. We want to finish reading a book, perhaps only to say we've finished it, or decide to eat up this bit of food to empty the container, or keep going on this jigsaw puzzle. We have a sense of accomplishment when we put in the last piece of the puzzle. Voilà!

In completing this puzzle, finishing this container of food, we don't think of all the other puzzles we have failed to complete, or to start, all the other containers, perhaps in other people's refrigerators, that we haven't finished. We may get quite exasperated if someone points this out: they're not ours! What we mean is: they weren't part of my project. But they haven't for that reason ceased to exist.

Our pleasure in finishing up a structure is based on a limitation of our viewpoint. Completing one structure means failing to complete, or start, countless others.

2.1 The projects that form the pattern of our life overlap.

We may think of them as being arranged in a pyramid. We are probably most conscious of the smallest, most momentary projects, like getting the newspaper, or reading it, or finishing our coffee. These are the small stones that form the base of the pyramid. Because they're changing all the time, being completed and replaced, we're conscious of them cumulatively. They create most of the short-term motion of our lives.

When we die, many of these projects remain unfinished. (See 0.7.) Those who come to clean up our house the day we are, say, taken to the hospital with a heart attack will find the dirty dishes in the sink, still sticky with oatmeal, the notice of the meeting we now won't be able to go to, and unwatered plants.

2.11 Death is an acceptable excuse for not doing the things we should have done. They were projects only for us. No one holds it against us that we have not read the paper if we are dead.

We are like Kakfa's suppliant in "Before the Law," for this reason an accurate parable of our self-imposed projects that seem so necessary to us, and yet are completely meaningless to others.[10] When the suppliant dies, the door to the Law, before which he has waited all his life hoping to influence the gatekeeper, is closed. Our goals and the actions we took to attain them, the rituals we undertook to get through the day in an ordered fashion, were only for us; now they may be abandoned.

2.12 The attainment of mid-level goals takes more time than any single momentary one: this is what makes the mid-level goals mid-level goals. These can be things like looking for a new house, or finishing a report at work that spans many months or even years. Even longer-term than that are such things as getting children through high school, or college. At the top is the largest plan of all: retirement, perhaps, a second house, a round-the-world trip.

2.121 Frequently, despite our best attempts, we fail to achieve goals, and drop them in favor of others. This produces a pattern of branchings off of branchings that leaves us a long way from the place we thought we were going to be when we look back on them.

This is probably what Frost meant in "The Road Not Taken."[11] When the traveler of the poem looks at the two roads, wondering which to take, he really can't tell which is better. The second isn't clearly preferable to the first, merely "just as fair." Nor was it clear that one was in fact "less traveled by," though this is what he knows he will say it was when he looks back from the distance of old age. Now, he admits that "as for that, the passing there/ Had worn them really about the same." However when he's old he'll look back on this choice and sigh, "knowing how way leads on to way." He may even try to justify this essentially arbitrary choice by feeling like Frank Sinatra singing "I Did It My Way": he'll be saying, with a sigh: "I took the road less traveled by." But the conviction that one has gotten where one is as the result of resolute action as an intrepid loner, he probably realizes (this may be the meaning of the sigh), is the calming delusion of old age. Instead, he merely chose at random.

2.13 For only a very few people does the end of life coincide perfectly with the achievement of all goals. And if by some chance we are one of the very few who has everything s/he wants when s/he dies, others probably feel sorry for us that we didn't have the chance to enjoy all we'd gained.

For some of us, late middle age and old age consist of a constant series of having to abandon our projects. We play our last game of basketball and now sit on the sidelines. We take our last drive in the car. If we are lucky, we find things we can still do and busy ourselves with them. Large projects give way to small. Perhaps our largest project is watching a bud on the plant on the windowsill. Will today be the day it blooms?

2.131 Some people live moment to moment, as if perennially at the base of the pyramid. But they still have projects, even if these are almost exclusively short-term ones.

2.14 Without goals, we don't have the sense of moving forward.

In his "Ode on a Grecian Urn," John Keats contrasts a carved boy chasing a carved girl to the flesh and blood version of the same thing.[12] The urn boy is frozen in time and so can never catch the girl. A flesh and blood boy, by contrast, can kiss the girl. In life, the boy achieves his goal. But, Keats implies, the time will come when he doesn't want it any more, precisely because he's already got it. In some ways the boy on the urn who can never kiss the girl is happier than the real boy who can achieve his goal (at which point it ceases to be one)—because he always has a goal.

We say that the point of goals is achieving them, but in fact, Keats reminds us, the point is having them.

2.15 We conceive of going forward with respect to the project, not with respect to other things. (See 2.03.) What we call "progress" in our lives is returning to our office and continuing to work on completing the same article, or by adding a few feet a day to the same roof, or the same road, or more rows to our piece of knitting, or another stamp to our album. If our project consists of six roads, we can add a foot a day to each of six, or six feet to one. Once having postulated the project, we can fill in the outlines any way we want. We think of this as creativity.

2.151 However we seem to have limited concentration powers: adding six feet to one road is probably better than adding a foot to each of six roads. Either of these is better than adding one foot to one road, then walking around, then looking at the sky, then working on your family's genealogy. We don't have a concept that unites all these disparate things, so they don't constitute a "project."

2.152 Scholars go back over and over to considering a specific Whatever (Mozart symphony, Mayan temple) rather than picking up something else. This makes them, we tend to agree, More Learned, whereas working on many things in succession would be held to be mere time-wasting.

Yet no one continually works on anything: the sensation that we do so is a fact of perception. We say: "I am working on James Joyce." Neither lunch nor the haircut counts as part of the project, nor the delicious E. F. Benson novel we read in the evenings, and possibly enjoy more. Nor do we have any way of giving greater or lesser value to the possible ways this sentence, "I am working on X," could be finished. "I am working on *Finnegans Wake*" seems as valid a project as "I am working on Section X of *Finnegans Wake*." So long as we have a name for "what I'm working on," we have a plan, and a goal. We have a project.

2.1521 "Joyce" is a project, perhaps one that can power a scholar's whole career. But what counts as a scholarly project, a legitimate object of knowledge, isn't something we determine: it's determined by what the world currently thinks is a project of knowledge. And this can change. "Authors who went blind" is not a project, unless we make it one. Doing so involves changing the world.

2.1522 Fields in scholarly study come to be and die. While they flourish, they allow coherence by elimination. No field as yet includes "squishy things on my front porch." But these things exist as much as anything else. Even the insistence that, say, many things escape "fields" can itself become the field of study.

2.2 In the pursuit of any project, the project only forms the over-structure. Everything underneath this comes along for the ride.

2.21 In brushing my teeth, the only part of the action that's determined by the project is brushing my teeth. Not the precise motions, the kind of toothpaste, the way I spit (or don't), the grimaces I make at myself in the mirror.

2.22 If my project is defined as getting from Washington, D.C. to New York, I can take the train or drive. (This is not so if my project is "taking the train from Washington, D.C. to New York.) If I drive, I can think many thoughts or listen to music while I do so. Some people prefer the train because they accomplish the goal and have room for many other kinds of things at the same time, like moving about. These are undetermined by the project of "getting to New York." Do them or not, the project is unaffected.

2.221 The degree to which the project occupies my mind changes. Long-term projects leave room for many things not directly determined by the project.

Between our respites from projects and the filler material that forms the body of projects, we have many opportunities to be aware of the vast unorganized body of the world.

2.222 Projects contain sub-projects, and overlap, as the different layers of the pyramid both support and presuppose one another.

My momentary project, let's say brushing my teeth, is part of my larger project of getting to work on time, which in turn is (say) part of my larger project of (say) retiring early and moving to Nevada. At any given time it may be complicated to articulate all the projects that are being pursued. But since projects are things we consciously set as goals, we are likely to be able to list a good number of them.

2.23 The projects which, piled into a pyramid that shapes our life, can also be visualized as a road map of narrow pathways snaking across an otherwise impassible jungle. The pathways are much smaller than the jungle, though they are what fill our consciousness.

2.24 If we have no projects, life contains too many data. Why do one thing rather than another? We have to have a path through the jungle. Otherwise we are overwhelmed with foliage.

From the perspective of the jungle, or someone in it, we may be going in circles.

2.25 Someone else's project might involve precisely the things that to us are distractions from our projects. Is being in a movie "work" or is it "play"? Movie actors speak of their "work" and are sometimes paid great sums. Yet non-actors pay money, or accept not getting money, for brief walk-ons in movies. Restaurant reviewers are getting money for eating the meal we pay for, theater critics get their tickets for free and are paid for the ensuing article, baseball players are paid to do what we amateurs think of as a free-time activity. And an artist might make something out of the tiles in the floor that normally we do not consider worth noticing. These turn into an end in itself something that usually is not part of the project.

2.251 Sometimes daydreamers end up making a great contribution to the world. They were not controlled by the paths of other people and so struck out on their own.

2.2511 Most daydreamers simply get lost in the jungle.

2.2512 The fact that someone is "marching to a different drummer" is sometimes held as evidence that what s/he is doing is of value. In fact most such people disappear with no trace. Yet their path without others felt the same to them as the paths without others of the innovators whom we later celebrate.

2.26 The limitation of our attention to a few things at a time allows us to have a sense of control over our lives. But this is only possible because we have already eliminated 99.99% of the other possibilities.

This means, we focus on the .01% of the world that remains.

2.261 If we focus (say) on the undeniable fact that we spend our lives between one excretion and another, between one need for sleep and another, and are each day brought one day closer to our graves (in the words of Shakespeare's Friar Lawrence), life seems dreary indeed. We could see ourselves as prisoners in a holding pen, some of whom, each day, are taken from the cell and slaughtered before our eyes. Some people have seen the human condition this way.

2.2611 Our world-view is determined not by what is true, but by what we place primary to other things. Other people than Friar Lawrence are growing old; for him death is paramount, though not for them.

People argue as if the people they are arguing with fail to acknowledge the existence of things. Probably the others are well aware that these other things exist; they are simply lower in the second person's rankings than they are in the rankings of the first. Change is subsidiary to permanence for one person; for another it may be the reverse. How can one of them hope to convince the other s/he is wrong?

2.262 We are unaware of being unaware of what we're unaware of. Usually we are unaware of the limitation of our point of view, precisely because we fail to consider the things we are failing to consider. (See 0.32.)

The world is full of unasked questions, undefined paths, unarticulated expectations.

2.263 The core of truth at the center of Michel Foucault's vast project is the realization that doing one thing means not doing many others.[13] Everything is defined by relation with what it isn't.

The over-reach of Foucault's epigones has been the notion that those doing one thing are engaged in the project of actively suppressing all they are not doing, rather than merely devoting themselves to the thing they are doing at the expense of the rest. Foucault's minions have made the world seem intent on grinding others down.

2.264 In doing A, we are failing to do X and Y. But it is the very pointing this out that brings this information to the table. Usually Foucauldians are furious that those doing A are not doing X or Y, and worse, not even admitting that they are not doing X and Y. But usually they aren't "not doing X or Y," they are simply failing to do X and Y. At the same time, as Foucauldians rarely admit, they are equally failing to do B, and C, among others, whose voices will still go unheard even if those of X and Y are heard. Indeed, B and C fail to be heard precisely because we are suddenly listening to X and Y, ignored (or ground down) in their turn.

2.265 When the cacophony of voices being heard is complete, we will be unable to hear ourselves think.

2.27 The more we are aware of the project, the more difficult it is to be aware of the things not related to the project or those subsumed under it. (See 0.32.)

When we sit in the car chafing at a red light (perhaps we are late for an appointment, or for taking our children to school), we do not see the millions of things around us we could be interested in. Over there is an especially well-maintained '50s car. In the nearby parking lot is a strange looping of shinier asphalt thrown like a Jackson Pollock painting over the regular white lines of the parking spaces. By the side of the road is a tree turned perhaps by a blight to a strange combination of unrelated halves, withered brown on one side and lush green on the other.

Instead of seeing these things and being interested by them, our whole being is taken up with counting the seconds till the light changes.

This doesn't mean we're stunted as human beings. It just means we're concentrating on our project.

2.28 Most of us define our largest projects the way others around us define theirs. We all want to be (say) CEO of the corporation, or a rock star, or at least are interested in the people who are these things, merely because they are. Or we want to be "famous." Why?

2.281 Mass-market thrillers in the U.S. turn around the phrase: The President is in Danger! No one would read a book that turns around the phrase: The Man Who Cleans Floor 14 is in Danger! Yet he may be more interesting, or more original, or better looking than the man who is President. What he is not is President.

It doesn't help to say: "I'm as good-looking as that movie star." The fact is, I'm not a movie star: people don't look at me, but instead at the star. But if the camera's attention were lavished on us, we would be the star instead.

2.2811 The whole phenomenon of "tipping points" turns around the fact that the very vocabulary for our projects comes from the public world.[14] Things are not the thing to have or do, until suddenly they are.

People want the one gadget others have, not because others have it, but because that is the gadget to have.

2.2812 Skeptics have described this phenomenon as "doing what others do" or "keeping up with the Joneses." But those who set these goals for themselves do not see themselves as keeping up with the Joneses. Instead, they see themselves as setting the goal whose desirability has been made clear by the fact that others are setting that goal too.

This is the source of the phenomenon of "winner take all" that was noted in the late twentieth century: one brand name, one opera singer, one whatever will be completely in demand, and all the others, no matter how well they fulfill the same goal, are not in demand. [15]

We are condemned to want what others want because they want it. But they want it because others want it too. What if each individual person withdrew his or her desire? Would the desired object change? Yes. It wouldn't be desired. In that sense it wouldn't be the same object.

2.282 Happiness works like real estate values, which are based on "comparables." A house is compared to a same-sized house in a nearby street that sold recently. We are happy or not depending on how well we measure up to what we take as our comparables, what we compare ourselves with.

2.283 We can change what we compare ourselves with. But we have to have a reason to change.

Usually we determine our comparables by our perception of who is involved in the same project or a similar one. We put ourselves in the same category as people of our age and education. Do we make less money than our business school classmate? We are likely to be cast down, unless we reason that he is not our comparable because he lives, say, in New York and we in the country. Do we make less money than the Queen of England? We are not likely to care, because she is not one of our comparables.

2.284 The paradox is that the more intent on our projects we are, the more likely we are to see only the one or two people closest to us, and be dissatisfied. We will never feel lucky that we are better off than all the rest.

It takes a consciousness of the world outside our projects to compare ourselves with, the less fortunate, and for that reason feel blessed. Say, with people in 1990s Rwanda. In comparison with lying dead in a ditch, we are all fortunate. To think this way we have to know about Rwanda, and not merely the boardroom of our corporation, our academic department, or the people in the cubicles closest to ours at work. This has to seem a real comparison to us.

What do we do if Rwanda is too far away from the people around us to seem real or be a comparable? Who is right and who wrong? Us or them?

2.285 We see only the one or two people hot on our heels and so are dissatisfied. We fail to see that we are ahead of all the others, or if we know it, we can get no satisfaction from this fact.

2.286 Yet we can become aware of all these others we are ahead of, and our dissatisfaction that there is one of our comparables ahead of us vaporizes, at least for a time.

2.287 Our feelings are determined what our comparables are at any given moment.

Seeing the world outside the paths we've chosen

2.3 For most of our lives, we remain on the pathways of our projects. They are the web we have spun for ourselves, and a spider travels on the threads of its web.

2.31 Even spiders can suddenly drop a line and leave the web. It is possible to jump the tracks on which we move forward.

2.311 Under certain circumstances we can de-couple ourselves from the track to which we are otherwise bound. Suddenly we can "smell the flowers." Even if those flowers are in fact car exhaust, the patterns of shiny black patching on the roadway, and the sultry feel of the heavy air in summertime Washington, D.C., suddenly they are there to be perceived, where before they weren't.

Stopping at a red light gives us a greater chance at suddenly being aware of the world that is not organized into our driving projects than rolling along, because it inserts a period of enforced idleness.

We are more likely to be aware of the crickets at night as we drift off to sleep than of the cicadas during the daytime, which are what we think of as "work hours." When we are focused on our projects, we are closed to random stimuli.

When we allow ourselves to drift, we are abruptly capable of sensing the whole world around us, which presents itself to us in sudden profusion. Indeed, it is in such profusion that we may realize why we limit our perception with projects.

The realization of the profusion of stimuli we're typically unaware of may cause vertigo: we realize that only we determine our projects. Their solidity is due to us, not a justification for our taking them as projects.

2.312 Sometimes we are forced from our pathways brutally and must somehow piece together our lives again: we are fired, a parent dies, or our spouse leaves us. Suddenly we perceive whole chunks of the world we hadn't seen before.

Or we visit a nursing home and discover a world of ticking clocks, of people sitting in chairs, waiting for the next meal, or the next visit. The meaning of time here is completely different than in our own lives! We may realize for the first time that there is nothing absolute about our projects.

Or we escape a traffic accident. This was something that didn't happen. We are aware of it in a way we are hardly ever aware of the millions of things that, at every moment, fail to happen. We think: how easily our projects could have been otherwise.

2.3121 Frequently our projects consist of putting things back the way they were before, as after an accident, after a storm, after a war. There is nothing particularly sacrosanct about the way they were before, yet our actions are determined by the fact that this is the way they were. We repair a vase, or re-build a city: what if it had been other than it was to begin with? What is the value of having things as they were? Merely that that's how they were. Re-creating the accidental becomes our project.

2.31211 Let's say we immerse ourselves, or find ourselves immersed, in the culture of a completely different people. Their goals are not our goals. Suddenly we see the pattern of our own pathways. Compared with what they ignore in our own lives, they seem absolute. Compared to others' goals, they seem relative.

2.3122 At this point we may ask, despairingly, what the sense of life might be.

Asking this question means we can never answer it. It's always a rhetorical question. Asking it means, we have come to the edge of our own lives.

2.3123 This is an abyss. We have to back up; we cannot go forward.

2.3124 To avoid this sense of the abyss, we can always look at others' patterns and subsume them to our own: our ways are the right ones, theirs are wrong. This sense of reaching the edge of an abyss is known only to those who see other people as being like themselves, rather than aliens.

2.3125 Those who conceive of the world in terms of right and wrong actions rather than people like themselves are not bothered by sensing difference: any divergence from the correct action is simply wrong.

2.3126 Let us say we are forced off the pathways of our projects. For many of us, the world off the tracks of our projects suddenly seems overwhelming: we are no longer moving forward, and feel lost in the underbrush.

"Coping" consists of getting back on the pathways, pretending we have the projects until once again we re-shoulder the burden, put our nose to the grindstone, and once again begin moving forward.

2.32 Other people keep us focused on our projects.

Most of us are rarely alone, so we tend to remain focused on our projects.

2.321 Other people require interaction according to social rules, which are usually related to our projects. Being alone sometimes encourages us to slip the traces of our action patterns, merely to graze, to get off the moving highways of our projects.

2.4 There are disadvantages to being completely focused on our projects.

If we're unaware that most of the world isn't marked with paths at all, we are also likely to be unaware of the possibility of taking a different path than the one we are on, or of the possibility of striking out on our own. Thus we doggedly do the same thing when it may long since have ceased to be effective.

2.41 Those concentrating on their own particular paths have little in common with those not on the same paths.

2.42 Others may see us on our ribbons of superhighways speeding along, clutching the wheels, and be amused by our strange intensity. We cannot be amused, for we are too focused on the tail of the car in front of us. To us the intensity isn't strange.

2.43 Being male in our society has traditionally been associated with being full of projects, striding purposefully forward. Consciousness of what the projects failed to consider was considered female.

2.431 In a gender-apportioned society, it has been the women who were allowed to perceive the rest of the world. This is why it was women who were associated with the arts.

2.432 We reduce individual unhappiness if people can decide which category they want to belong to. Instead of saying, the men take care of the world organized into projects, and the women take care of the way things look, we have learned to say: the balance between moving forward and perceiving the world is something an individual needs to strike.

2.44 In times of threat, the projects take over. During a defense crisis, only the military matters. During a health crisis, personal or collective, it seems that nothing is more important than the doctors. But once they have kept us safe and alive, what then? The doctors will not save us from boredom or make us happy, and we were alive before the military kept us so. Then the old questions re-surface.

Frustration

2.5 Frustration is the identification of where we are vs. where we want to be, the world vs. the path we want to be on.

If I am stuck in traffic while I ought to be at a sales meeting, I can become frustrated. If I have nowhere to go, I am much less likely to be frustrated.

2.51 We avoid frustration by re-negotiating the relationship between our path and the things it passes over.

2.511 We have only to re-define our project to be in sync with the world again. Perhaps, getting there by 4 o'clock rather than 3, or getting home in one piece.

2.512 We can also take action, say find another road. This isn't always possible.

2.52 Those who learn to "let go and let God" risk giving up their projects entirely. But this does reduce frustration to close to zero.

2.521 We don't get frustrated unless we see clear alternatives to what is happening.

2.522 We don't curse the world that there is not a more direct route to our goal than the one there is, unless we can visualize it. We say we can go around this way or that way, but going through the building is not something we consider, unless we have a machine that goes through the building.

2.523 There is no more direct route than the most direct route there is. Unless we set out to make a yet more direct route.

2.524 All works, all actions of people who change things come from seeing something that, in the eyes of others, isn't there: a more direct route, a better mouse trap. To outsiders looking on, it seems to come from nowhere. To the person him- or herself, it was as clear as day.

2.525 Ultimately we all must simply accept, and cease looking for routes around: for instance with our own death, and probably many times before. Our job is to accept what has happened, not to avoid it or fix it.

Magic

2.53 The situation that produces frustration is the same situation that produces the desire for magic. We want to be able to wave a wand and have the traffic disappear, or to be able to go through the building.

Magic is what would get us something we want but see no way to get. The desire for it is created when we have identified a gulf between project and world. This is always a specific gulf, and the result of our projects.

We don't see a possible solution, so we postulate one: this would be the magical solution. Magic is our wild card when things can't get any worse.

Magic thus goes beyond the possible. Is it itself "possible"? It's as justified to say it is as to say it isn't. Saying it is leads to the belief that magic is another realm, always waiting for us. Yet magic isn't another realm than our own; it's the sum total of what we evoke on a case-by-case basis that would solve problems in this realm.

2.531 Magic, if it solved the problem it's invoked to solve—if our Fairy Godmother suddenly appeared—would in any case only solve a particular problem.

If we wish for a third arm, and get it, there will be a circumstance where we need a fourth. If magically we had the power to read minds, that would be our new reality, which would require the next level of problem solving that would be the magic of this new reality.

2.532 The magic worked in the Harry Potter books is so predictable because it solves only the problems of the "muggles," those of us caught in human reality.[16] Harry's magic is defined by the things that frustrate us, not him. If everyone were a wizard, they'd in fact be the muggles of their world. Who's to say we're not already the wizards of another one-step-down world? And do we rejoice in our powers? We are only interested in the things we can't do, not the things we can.

2.533 Ghosts are scary only because we are who we are: our limits are what make them strange, because they are postulated as transcending these limits— death, the body. But ghosts, if they exist, will also have limits. The question becomes, what will haunt the ghosts?

Ghosts are scary because that's the role they play in our lives. We have made them so.

2.6 The uncharted world is the only part of the world that we can find interesting in its own right. Things we have made part of our projects become merely emanations of our own actions. Pursuing them may be exhilarating, but it cannot change us in any way.

2.61 The choice is binary: either we make the world ours by folding it into our projects, or we sense the world as existing independently of us. We can't have both of these simultaneously.

The either/or nature of this choice comes from the fact that actions we are taking mean we are responsible for what happens. What we are responsible for is not something we can find solid. It is only a means to our ends.

2.62 The chef cannot eat his own dinner with the same degree of enjoyment as a diner in the restaurant, for whom it simply appears. The chef judges his dinner, the diner appreciates it. The man who has built his own house may well be proud of his handiwork, but he cannot see it as the realm of mystery that his children will, or even as the solid object that a guest may perceive. We say, he knows too much about it.

2.621 Similarly, it is difficult for us to love someone we know too much about.

2.63 We cannot actually ever achieve the thing we want, because when we get it we no longer want it.

2.631 When we say we want something so badly we can taste it, the taste is merely its relationship to ourselves, and to not having it.

2.6311 It may have no taste at all for someone else.

We should beware of thinking that others around us—say, our children, our students—will share our desires.

2.6312 When we get the thing we wanted, it changes from something we wanted so badly to something we possess. It will lose that taste.

Childhood

2.7 The beauty and power of childhood comes from the fact that the world seems solid in childhood. Because we are so impotent, we are free to experience absolutely. If we were powerful, we would see the world as something we control, and so it would not offer itself to us absolutely. Instead, it would be absolutely contingent.

The young are not responsible for the world, and so they experience it.

2.71 Most of us long to become adults, but we lose something along the way that we can only find again, vicariously, in other children, perhaps our own. We enjoy seeing something "through a child's eyes," or "being a child again."

An advertisement on a Washington, D.C. area radio station asks listeners to think of the way summers used to be: freedom from school, no books, lazy summer afternoons. Recapture that feeling, it urges us. Go to a certain chain of ice cream parlors.

Yet of course we can never recapture the delicious drift of childhood summers, because now we are where our parents were, or perhaps even grandparents. We are the ones who make the summers possible. Only our children can enjoy them the way we once did. Now we are the ones paying for the ice cream, and driving the car that gets us there.

2.72 We can revisit our old haunts, but they are never the same. We had no idea they were so ordinary, the house like all the other houses on the block. This is what Thomas Wolfe's famous title *You Can't Go Home Again* means to most people.[17]

In my mind's eye I can still see the slope, not more than a few inches, up to the neighbor's yard, the pale new grass of spring lined up by the tines of the rake against the dark earth beneath like the sparse hair of a cancer patient. Or the gray crabapple tree with four twisting branches coming up like fingers from an imperfect hand and leaving a palm to sit in, the bars of solid light falling through the windows of an empty garage and filled with the dancing motes of chinchilla-fine dirt from the floor.

A stranger, seeing these things, would look, and look away. Even I cannot believe they were once so important. Only in memory do they retain the power of the absolute, not a layer that can be torn away to make room for another, but the flesh and blood of the retina itself.

2.73 Adulthood comes in realizing that each thing that seemed so absolute to us had alternatives: the house we lived in was merely the house our parents chose, or could afford, or were forced to live in. Thus the peculiar pattern of boards that creaked, or of stains in the rug, or nails in the wall, that meant so much to us as children, has no particular value, except to us, being identical in all respects save their very particularity with the particularities of every other house in our block, and the next, and the next city.

No one knows these things but us, if we were an only child, or the surviving sibling. Whom to share them with? Ultimately no one wants the things most important to us. This is one of life's great tragedies.

2.731 As children we know only one set of things, and do not conceive of them as being instances of types. Instead, they are absolute. We have not a mother, but Mommy, not a father but Daddy, not a small ranch house on a cul-de-sac but Home.

2.732 In childhood the world consists of a handful of huge surfaces, like great countries on a map filling a continent. We have no control over them, save insofar as they present alternatives to each other.

2.733 As we grow up, we shatter these huge surfaces, subdividing, destroying empires. We also reduce house, room, school, and parents in size to make room for many other things. As a result we are able to move them about more easily, compare one to the next. They no longer fill most of the board.

2.74 As the owner of a house, we see the house as the result of actions we have undertaken. It takes on the tracks of actions in the world. The paint is merely a color chosen among others, or something that must be re-done next year. The gutters have to be cleaned quarterly, and the driveway probably needs new stone.

I am the master of the stones in my driveway. Thus I am unlikely to pore over them, looking for strange shapes, in the way my four-year-old son, who is their servant, can do.

2.75 We can never find solid the things or beings of which we are the master. This is true in literal terms, and leads to the prison of colonial experience, captured so well by George Orwell in his essay "Shooting an Elephant" and his novel *Burmese Days*.[18] We must impress those we define as our inferiors, we cannot merely interact with them. Nor can we enjoy them.

2.76 For those with what we think of as truncated childhoods, say who had to look out for smaller siblings at an early age, childhood holds none of the beauty it does for most of us. Like Emma Bovary—who Flaubert said knew so much about the farm from having grown up there that she was immune to the nostalgia of the city folks for the rural—such people see only actions to be taken, contingencies rather than the perceptual absolutes that usually typify childhood.

2.77 Proust managed to find thousands of pages to write about the smallest details of his childhood experience.[19] But this unusual access to childhood experience came at a price most of us are unwilling to pay. His ability to re-live his childhood was only possible because he was such an inactive adult, by the standards of most of the world. His adult life past a certain point *was* the evocation of his childhood.

Most of us cannot mentally regain our childhoods, at least not in the profusion of a Proust. We have a sense of childhood being a lost world we can never regain, and catch it in mere whiffs when we open a box of birds' nests, or a stamp collection stored in the attic.

2.78 Wordsworth wrote in his "Ode: Intimations of Immortality" about how, as we grow older, the world fades "into the light of common day." He thought that the magic of childhood was the result of faint remembrances of having come from a better place than Earth: "trailing clouds of glory do we come." Then we figure out how things work, and become actors ourselves. The poet summarized growing up by saying that "Shades of the prison-house begin to close/ Upon the growing boy."[20] This is not a positive view of adulthood.

Growing up and changing

2.8 Growing up means accepting the fact of change. That means, knocking askew the things that seemed so solid in our pasts, prying them away from their bases and merely setting them back where they were before. The field next door is now a strip mall. The house on the corner has been torn down.

The first time we have to process change, the experience is upsetting. We merely swallow the hurt, we cannot avoid it.

2.81 The realization that any of the faces of life can shatter and be replaced with a picture of itself is the sign of adulthood. The surface looks the same, but we know it is not solid.

2.811 This is the subject of some of Magritte's paintings.[21]

2.82 Our children, for whom the strip mall was a given, will not sense this same feeling of melancholy and transience.

2.83 Life consists of a continuous series of getting used to changes. This means, a continuous knocking off center and re-attachment. But the re-attachment is never as strong the second, or the third, or the subsequent times. All of us are like a piece of sticky tape: if only we could have stayed where first we were attached!

2.84 Pity the poor Cumean Sybil. Her mournfulness was the mournfulness of constant change. *Semper aliquid novi.*[22] What a horror!

2.85 Usually we are given time to digest changes as they come one by one. But think of when we return to a place we have left years before and recognize almost nothing: it is too much, we have to un-stick so many solid things.

2.86 Children, for whom the new is the given, the absolute, find it comical when their parents sigh for the past. One day the children will sigh for this present, become their own pasts.

2.87 To a degree, the past, even the recent past, or that of adulthood, is like childhood. We are not responsible for it.

Because we are no longer moving along the paths, we can go back and realize what the path, and the area around it, looked like. We are free to see it as if from the outside.

2.88 Sartre thought the structure of the past, which was absolutely given, was intrinsically different from that of the future, which was purely contingent. It was solid, the way, for him, other people are solid.[23]

2.881 The past is not another structure than the future. Both are marked by the relationship of project to what the project fails to consider, path to jungle.

The future is not absolutely different from the past. The future has some of the same "drag" as the past because we have projects, which to be sure we can alter or give up.

2.882 Because Sartre thought the undetremined future was absolutely different than the fixed past, this binary contrast required him to "outlaw" the projects, the things that prove him wrong. This is the source of his resistance to projects, which after all give a pattern to life, make it possible. If I undertake actions merely to complete a project, this for Sartre is "bad faith."

2.883 It is not possible to live without "bad faith," because this is what gives shape to our lives. Otherwise we are lost in the undifferentiated profusion of sensations.

2.89 For Sartre the openness of the future was the result of being flung forward into existence. All people, he held, are free.

Sartre is right that living our freedom is the most difficult thing of all. Yet in fact it is so difficult, not to mention such a bad idea, that there is nothing to recommend it.

Parents and children

2.9 The perception of parents and children of their common world is fundamentally different.

2.91 The parents remember when the child was not. For the parents, the child belongs to them, was made by them. The child has no such perspective.

2.92 Children take for granted the things their parents made possible for them, because this is all they have ever known. The child of parents who worked for what they have cannot see all they have acquired as an alternative to anything. It was around for as long as they can remember.

The parents may make an effort to convince the children that wealth has alternatives, perhaps by making the child work, or having the child contribute to his or her upkeep. This can succeed to the extent of "giving the child an appreciation" for what the parents did for them, but if there is no serious danger of not having the wealth, the experience of the child cannot be that of the parents.

2.93 Frequently parents tax children with "ingratitude." Of course the children cannot be grateful in the way the parents want, because they have nothing to compare what they know with.

2.931 Parents press small children to their warm bodies to give them love. They give them food. It therefore seems to parents that the adult these children turn into will be closer to them than anyone else. As a result they are shocked by the divergences between themselves and their children.

2.9311 They are not shocked by much greater divergences between themselves and a distant acquaintance, much less between themselves and someone they don't know who is halfway around the Earth.

2.9312 Here, as so often, expecting more means we have the sense of getting less. In the same way, our most intense arguments are by definition with people whose positions are closest to our own: we are fighting for the same turf.

2.932 Our children never see us the way we see ourselves. Another person from a completely different milieu may be able to. This person will be the one most like us.

2.933 It's as if parents and children talk different languages. They understand each other through gestures, if at all.

2.94 The love of parents for children is, typically, unconditional: whoever the child is, the parents will love him or her. But this means that the love is not of the individual. Which is why the child, on growing older, will typically search out someone who loves him or her for him- or herself. And so the cycle continues.

2.941 Parents are part of the givens, the absoluteness, of the world. They merely are.

2.9411 The love of parents and children is asymmetrical. The children will never love the parents with the unconditional love that their parents had for them, because they take the parents for granted. Parents do not take children for granted, because they remember the time when the children did not exist.

Parents love children because they feel they are responsible for the children. Children do not feel responsible for the parents.

2.942 The love of the child for the parents may seem to the parents to be a love of them as individuals. In fact it's merely an attachment to the person who defines their world. Later this may be re-negotiated as the child sees that the parent is only a person among other people.

2.9421 The child may understand intellectually that without the parents s/he would not be alive, but given that s/he is alive, the parents do not seem particularly involved. No wonder patriarchal societies like the ancient Hebrews felt it necessary to admonish children to honor their parents.

2.95 Parents typically want control of their children. Because they have created these children, they feel the children belong to them. Given all they have done for the children it seems, in all fairness, the children should serve them.

2.951 Some societies place a premium on doing what the parents, more typically the father, wants. But even in such societies—the Confucian Chinese, the ancient Greek—the son's subservience to the father rarely outlived the father himself, with the child feeling liberated at the death of the father.

2.952 Freud made the "Oedipal conflict" part of a larger scheme of elaborate theories.[24] As is frequently the case in Freud, the kernel of his intuition seems sound. It is intrinsically true that sons will frustrate fathers who want the sons to see things the way they, the fathers, do. Thus the more obedience the father demands, the more certain is a large degree of tension.

This is a structural danger, but it's only statistically probable. There's nothing to say it will be produced in every individual father/son relationship. Yet Freud suggests it is.

The disadvantage of Freud's insistence on psychologizing his theories is his unwieldy insistence that they did too work out in each individual case. He could have left them as literary or philosophical intuitions: if the shoe fits, wear it. But no. Freud felt it necessary (was this his own power play?) to claim them valid for each and every person.

I may well like my father. But then Freud has to be ready to assume me that, despite what I say or believe, I really don't like him at all.

Shoring up the defenses of an untenable psychologizing thus becomes the lion's share of the theory: repression, the structure of the psyche to explain how it's even possible to deny what Freud asserted.

2.953 As a result of this, in Freud's world, things never are as they seem.

Freud's universe is a world of conflicts about to happen, or narrowly prevented from happening. Freud's theories always explain an apparent energy level of 0 as an underground force of -10 usually kept down by a force of +10. Sometimes the positive force slips up.

Those nay-sayers who, when Freudian thought was new, sensed that for Freud the normal was an exception to the pathological were correct. This is so because of the structure of his thought.

He could have identified and treated the pathological without sketching it as a version of the normal. But intellectually speaking this would have been a lot less interesting, because the claims would have more modest.

Thinkers always gain importance by making outlandish claims. If we made realistic ones, no one would listen to us. So instead of saying the sky is up, we say that the sky is down, and then insist upon this. People will talk about us now.

2.954 Because each person's project is merely each person's project, my father will ultimately be irrelevant to me. I am who I am. Fathers are ultimately beside the point for the son, though the father doesn't want to acknowledge this. This is the correct intuition at the center of Freud's theory.

2.9541 A father may be proud of having a son "just like him." But was he himself just like his own father? If so, the son is like the grandfather (or his father), not the father. If not, why should the father be perpetuated in a way his own father was not? And why stop the chain with the grandfather? At what point is it acceptable for the son to deviate from the father? If back then, why not now?

2.9542 What is the value of replicating ourselves if we ourselves are replications of something else?

2.9543 We speak nowadays of "passing on our DNA" as if there were some value to the particular pattern the kaleidoscope's bits fell into in this moment. We ourselves are by definition mongrels of many people's DNA. So too will our children be.

2.955 People rarely succeed in telling other independent actors what to do, at least past their own deaths, and must content themselves with dominating people who do not function as independent actors. In more traditional societies, this category can include women, or outsiders/slaves; in almost all societies it includes children.

Typically, the children whom their parents succeed in controlling past the grave are unable to be full actors in the world: the spinster daughter who dies a year or two after the mother with whom she has lived, the son so controlled by the father that he simply gives up and lives on a pale shadow of his father's will.

2.96 The entropy of child-rearing is cumulative, not individual. For this reason Freud's attempts to see the drama at the level of a single generational turn-over is misguided. We give to our children, who give to their children. Usually our children only understand what we have given to them when they have children of their own.

2.961 Successful parenting consists of letting out the reins gradually and then hanging them up. Our job is to make ourselves irrelevant.

Because this requires alteration, and attention to the moment—is this the right time? Is this?—it can rarely be negotiated without bumps or major blowups. One of the ways that children signal they are approaching the point where they must be given more freedom is by demanding it. This means, almost inevitably they demand it before they are quite ready for it. This fact leads to the give and take of child-rearing, the sense of constraint and freedom working out of sync.

This is what makes child-rearing so wearing from the parents' perspective.

2.97 Parents want children to be predictable. If children are predictable, parents don't have to worry about them.

This is therefore a selfish desire, more about the parents but not the children.

2.971 We can only predict another person based on the path of their projects, not on the things the path neglects. Each person has to find his or her own path. That's how s/he knows it's his or her own.

2.972 Children will not be more predictable than the parents themselves were.

2.973 Parents who become furious at their children doing things they, the parents, don't want the children to do should remind themselves that the proportion of predictable and foreseeable to unpredictable is miniscule. It's far more likely the children will be in unpredictable territory than in predictable.

2.98 Parents should assume their children are unlike them. That way they will be pleasantly surprised by any similarities.

How do we make our lives meaningful?

3 Meaning in life comes from perceiving the whole map of pathways and surrounding area.

3.01 The love of parents for young children is absolute love because we see the creation of their projects, those we impose and those the children come up with on their own. We see the whole map. With greater age, adolescence and adulthood, we lose the sense of seeing the whole map. We sense this as a loss.

3.011 In the love of another adult we sense someone from the outside. We get to know them. We get to know their map.

3.012 In being loved by another adult who has chosen us, we feel we are perceived as if from the outside and valorized. We cannot see what we do from the outside. We see ourselves reflected "in another's eyes" and see that what we do has a shape. We exist.

This is particularly necessary because our own map feels arbitrary to us.

3.013 It doesn't matter what the shape of our map is. What we see is the contrast between projects and the world from which they are taken.

3.0131 Sartre thought, like Descartes, that the division between ourselves and other people was absolute, a binary division.[25] This is not the case. Others form a scale with respect to us. There are people closer to us and people further away. Those closer to us know what some of the alternatives were to the path we ultimately took, or were forced to take. Or we know what some of the alternatives were for them. We feel close to them because they can understand our struggle. We can love them, or be loved.

3.0132 Strangers, or people further away, see increasingly only the path we took. To these people, it is as if we meant it this way all along.

3.0133 Parents are at the opposite end of a spectrum from strangers, but ultimately identical to them in one way: all accept almost any turning. In order to exchange love, we need more discerning judges.

3.02 For many people, the love of God is the most absolute love. We feel that whatever we do, God knows. God is watching us. We live our lives open to Him, as if on a stage for an audience of one.

3.021 Telling the story of our life makes us feel that our life made sense. This is true whatever we did, or did not do, in our life. Telling it makes its shape visible, which it was not while we were living it.

3.022 God sees our twistings and turnings as if in a story. He sees them the way we see snaking highways and the glowing patterns of buildings from an airplane. Whatever we do is part of the pattern of our lives.

3.023 To say that God loves us means that God is aware of us.

Vacations

3.1 All people need, if only occasionally, to get off the tracks of their projects and sit on the sidelines where the world is solid, and not merely emanations of themselves.

One way of getting off the tracks is through vacations and travel.

3.11 Some people seek the exotic. We perceive the exotic as a flat frieze, like childhood. It is something we do not control, and so is absolute. This is the definition of exotic, which means it can be anywhere.

If we tell ourselves a place we are in is foreign, we are not responsible for things that go on there. For some people, foreign may be as close as the next town. For most Americans, locked into mono-linguality, it is any country where the people do not speak English, or where the people have an "accent." Thus Anglophone Canada seems un-exotic to most Americans, and is also the reason why Francophone Canada plays up its Frenchness in tourist ads.

3.111 Proust's vast masterwork *In Search of Lost Time* is partly about the realization that all exotic places and things are only so because of our placement with respect to them. Most exotics are personal exotics, some are more generally shared.

3.1111 The intellectual's version of the search for the exotic is thinking the lives of artists and thinkers somehow more exotic than other lives. An actress with a false nose portraying Virginia Woolf in a movie about her loads her pockets with stones and walks into a river. The music swells. "I fear I shall go mad," says the voice-over, quoting the author.[26] How tragic!

For Virginia Woolf it was not tragic. It was the feeling of the stones, the inability to focus, the slipperiness of the mud, the first gulp of water. The exoticism is only in the music, the portrayal, the light glinting for the movie's viewer off the cinematic water: not in the way things were for the person herself. We find it fascinating because we are looking on, not the person doing this.

Perhaps viewers of the movie are inspired to read Virginia Woolf's works. These are about the ordinariness of the world as lived, its lack of any intrinsic charge or interest. Almost inevitably they find they enjoy them far less than the Hollywood movie that makes the author into a tragic character. Where is the swelling music? In the works themselves are only the string of sensations that Woolf knew to constitute life, and the frames of things such as insects or other people the author put around these sensations to give them shape.

The point of Woolf's fiction is that any taste we have in life comes from our distance from it. This is not a realization compatible with seeking the exotic, which is based on a belief in outside, objective meaning and taste, not what the individual constructs to keep from going mad.

3.112 The search of tourists for the quaint, the undiscovered, and the untouched that drives them to Borneo, New Guinea, and beyond, is not silly, as some commentators have tried to make it. It is the necessary expanding of the quotidian that interests us until we realize the next exotic will be identical to the previous one.

Of course this search for the exotic does use up the world, as people invade untouched places and touch them.

3.113 For Anglophones who rent a house in Provence or Tuscany, the very fabric of life is interesting. How quaint, the local way of doing things! The *baguettes et vin rouge*, the *pane e vino*. And to think that life can go on in a language we do not speak! Everything we see is interesting, like our memories of childhood. It is solid, absolute.

3.114 For those who live there, or who visit for too long, things are quite different, just as our parents never saw the old apple tree we played on as children the way we did.

They do not find their own language quaint, nor their food, nor the way things are. And they are involved in the complex nets of their own lives, which means that for them, the street is merely something that lets them get from point A to point B; their houses are the things that need repair and must be paid for.

3.1141 When we return to our own lives, it is like leaving the solid for the insubstantial. We cannot see our own lives in the solid way we see the exotic. Reality begins as the airplane touches down again at home.

3.1142 In our own lives, we see the car as a means to get us places, the street as a connection with work, and our houses as places to live in. They aren't foreign. They are functional.

3.115 In the exotic world, by contrast, everything is a surprise. Typically, intellectuals hate Disneyland because nothing is a surprise. Intellectuals have used up reams of paper complaining about Disneyland.

3.12 Many people like Disneyland. Disneyland is the other kind of vacation. It isn't exotic, but then again it isn't meant to be.

3.121 Some people never cease to define the world in terms of their projects. For them, a vacation is the illusion of having achieved their goals on the pathway.

The Disneyland vacation seeks a place further forward on the path rather than sideways into the uncharted wilderness, if only for a short time, and in exchange for money.

3.122 For such vacations, we go to a completely predictable place, or to a resort where we are treated as the dollar royalty we would like to be. The staff in the hotel are there for our comfort. Small things—shaken or stirred? Charbroiled or deep-fried?—take on cataclysmic proportions. The staff say to us, yes sir, and yes ma'am. We have succeeded beyond our wildest dreams: this is the pot of gold at the end of the rainbow. We have got it only by booking it.

Of course it isn't really the pot of gold we're looking for. But it is the only pot of gold we can book for a certain date.

3.123 Disneyland is like a resort on an impoverished tropical island: we know we will get what we want. There will be no unpleasant surprises, so long as we stay inside the gates of the resort and do not venture out onto the lanes of shacks. It too is the life we are aiming at.

To be sure, it isn't real. But neither is the exotic real. Both are vacations; neither is the real goal at the end of our real project. Yet if and when we get the real goal at the end of the project it won't taste the way we thought it would.

Vacations aren't our projects. That's what makes them vacations. They are not our world.

3.1231 On vacation, we are able to achieve the sense we had in childhood of drifting, seeing the world as a blank surface.

3.124 If we are too aware of this hotel or this resort as something we have created, albeit collectively rather than singly, it becomes merely another part of our project.

3.125 To be a successful vacation, it must give us the feeling of having been accidental. We arrived here as if by chance, and look how we were treated!

3.126 This is why the monetary exchange on which it is all predicated is minimized: only one bill, at the end, presented discreetly, or an entrance fee at the gate. We get this out of the way and then can imagine what we want.

3.127 Putting resort hotels in tropical third-world countries solves the problem of the weather, unless it is the rainy season. But it poses other problems. We have to be careful not to wander outside the bounds of the resort. Reality begins at the fence. Why come all this way if only for reality?

Celebrities

3.2 When not on vacation, we get respite from our projects only briefly and in flickers. Some of us get it relaxing in a chair with a beer at the end of the day. Some of us get it from watching television, all of which is created to get us watching—which is to say, get our dollars for the products advertised. As a result television is a continuous flattering of our beliefs about ourselves: it has to keep us tuned in. This is why we like it. If we didn't, it wouldn't be what it is.

Some of us get respite from our projects by being interested in the lives of celebrities.

3.21 Celebrities perform for us: everything they do is part if the performance. Do they smile and blow kisses? This is part of the performance. Do they stamp their feet and break cameras? This too is part of the performance. They are like the Pagliaccio from Leoncavallo's opera whose very wails of pain are thought to be part of his role; everything they do is interesting to us.[27]

3.22 Some people make the mistake of thinking that they want to *be* these celebrities. So glamorous! And so many people paying attention! But people don't really want to *be* the celebrities. They want to be themselves, wanting to be these celebrities. What can the celebrities themselves do with all the people looking at them?

Art

3.3 Art is related to life the same way a vacation is. It's real, but it's off the path of our projects. That's why we can enjoy it.

Several centuries of art theory have suggested that art is a parallel world to ours, an unreal one, perhaps even a "higher" one. This isn't so any more than it's so that magic is another realm: it's connected piece by piece to our own. Any transcendent realm is connected to the realm it transcends, through the fact of what it transcends.

There are many quite real aspects of a vacation: the weather must cooperate, the beds must be comfortable, and the food must be good. In an exotic world we can get dysentery or have other unpleasant experiences. The only unreal, or at least unusual, aspect of a vacation is that we are not confined to the tracks that usually constrain us. This isn't unreal at all: the reality is that we are not on the track of our projects.

In the same way, artworks are made of the body of the world, but can offer an alternative to it. Art is merely at a different place in the world, it is not a different sort of object.

It is true that we don't use art as part of our project. But this is a result of the fact that it's off our path. This location means that it's art, which is why we interact with art by merely perceiving it.

What we merely perceive is what we call art, defined by its location. Kant got the causality wrong in defining the beautiful as what we merely perceive.[28] It's true that the artistic part of an object, here the beautiful, is what we merely perceive, but this isn't what makes it art. Rather this is the effect of that part of the object being off the path of our projects.

3.31 Art is not a separate realm, any more than taking time out to "smell the flowers" is an act unrelated to the fact that most of the time we don't smell the flowers. We're only drawn to smell the flowers as an alternative to usually not doing so.

3.32 The distinction between fiction and non-fiction is a distinction of emphasis, not an absolute one. Most of the bulk of any fictional work is pure fact.

3.321 Art, like the rest of the world, must get its facts right. In a novel, people eat with knives and forks like in the real world, the sky is up and sometimes blue but rarely custard yellow (if it is there has to be a reason, as the sky in a Munch painting can be blood red); the Queen of England for most of the nineteenth century was named Victoria, not Nellie, and the northernmost country in North America is called Canada. Or at least it makes little sense to call it anything else if the country to its south is called the United States of America and the country to *its* south the United States of Mexico.

3.322 The facts art need get right are those the members of its ideal audience group will be able to correct it on. Thus all artworks have a specific relationship to the world.

We should speak here of an "ideal" audience rather than "intended" one because the makers of the work may not have thought of this as an issue at all.

We can have a novel about a woman named Jane Smith who worked as a chambermaid in Bath in 1876; we may not have a novel about Queen Nellie of England who reigned in the 1880s unless this is part of a larger pattern of social satire, the "error" committed knowingly for a larger purpose.

3.323 We know about Queen Victoria; we do not know about chambermaids in Bath. Chambermaids in Bath are situated in the gray area of our knowledge. We don't know for a fact that things weren't this way.

3.324 Eighteenth-century theory spoke here of the "plausible," as if this too were a separate realm. Plausible means simply we don't know.

3.33 Sometimes artworks, through what for one group is a "blooper," delineate their ideal audiences quite clearly. A Brian de Palma movie had its heroine involved in a lengthy sequence filmed in the Philadelphia Museum of Art, whose main staircase she descended—only to walk out into traffic on 5th Avenue, New York.[29] These rooms from Philadelphia were standing in for the Metropolitan Museum; if we saw that they weren't, we weren't the ideal audience of the movie. For people who don't go to many East Coast museums, the Philadelphia Museum and the Metropolitan are much the same. For those with more knowledge, this counts as a major mistake. We might be able to forgive one such mistake, but if the work is too littered with them, we turn away in disgust.

This is one way in which a work can be bad. If the blooper is at a fundamental level, the whole premise repulses us (a sadist whom we're meant to see as a fun-loving prankster, for example).

I read a Japanese novel in translation that wrote about the "University of Georgetown" in the United States, but it bore no resemblance to Georgetown University in Washington, D.C. Probably it was a mistake to translate this novel into English, or perhaps this point should have been altered in the translation.

Yet this probably worked all right for a Japanese audience, just as making up a small town in Wyoming would work all right in a Hollywood film—so long as its projected audience was not the county in Wyoming where this was set.

3.331 As a result Kant's fundamental premise that judgments of beauty—what constitutes art—could be shown to be generally shared, and this by definition. Here as in all things Kant shows the iron fist inside the velvet glove. What if we say that people's reactions come first, then we can sketch what they hold to be beautiful—rather than the reverse? It seems unlikely Kant will simply make an offended moue and leave us alone. Far more likely is, he'll try to show us just how wrong we are.

No philosophy is ever disinterested. The more it insists it is the more we should be beware.

3.3311 This philosophy is not disinterested. But by the same token, it doesn't pretend to be.

It says, over and over: consider your limitations.

Certainly some people will not want to consider their limitations. They will deny that they have limitations.

No one can prove them wrong.

3.34 We're not in a new realm of "the plausible" when we read about Becky Sharpe, we're in the uncharted area of our collective knowledge.[30]

We can read about Becky Sharpe without seeing a blooper because we don't have handy the mental list of all young women living around the time of the Battle of Waterloo.

3.341 Conversely, we object to biographies of people we have information on that fill in the blanks with things we know the writer does not have access to. An author will not know what Queen Victoria thought on a certain day unless she wrote down that she did, but Thackeray may tell us all he wishes about Becky Sharpe.

This is the reason writers make up characters. Most theoreticians have thought the making up was the most important part of the action. It isn't. The making up is in the service of producing a person about whom things can be said without fear of correction.

3.3411 We can do research to find out what Queen Victoria actually did say, eat, or even (if there are letters?) think. If these become general knowledge, the writer cannot make them up; s/he must follow what we know to be true. Of course, the result of the research may be, there is nothing to discover: we will never know. In this case we are free to make things up.

3.342 Authors have to know what is known if they want anybody but themselves to read their works.

3.343 Fiction combines things an audience can judge for truth with things it cannot, either because it lacks the ability to judge now or because it will always lack this ability. Sometimes we agree tacitly not to look for this information. We are pretty sure that Becky Sharpe won't be found on anyone's census rolls, so we don't even try to look for her. But if we researched the world she's said to have been in, it might begin to bother us that Thackeray wrote about someone we knew for a fact had never existed, in the same way it would bother us if he called Queen Victoria "Nellie." It would seem ridiculous, as a movie that shows actors "playing the violin" with the bow a half an inch off the strings while violin music pours from the screen seems ridiculous to real musicians.

3.344 Knowing more can change the boundaries of what counts as art. The boundary is always being re-negotiated.

3.4 Art functions by getting us off the tracks of our projects. For a time, it invites us to care about other things. Yet if they were part of our projects rather than merely sidelines, we couldn't enjoy them, we would have to deal with them. They would be part of the project rather than a respite from the project.

3.41 This is why Tosca's suicide off the Castel San Angelo affects us more than the death of real people in Central American mudslides.[31] Tosca is a real alternative to our lives. We pay attention to her. People in mudslides aren't alternatives, they're part of the same world as our projects, only too far away to matter.

3.411 Art is an alternative to our project. In a way we might say, it is the project of leaving our project.

Art functions like going to the dentist. There is a face looming in front of ours, but we do not interact with it. We feel so close to Tosca because we know all about her, yet we don't have to interact with her following societal rules.

3.412 Aristotle thought tragedy inspired pity and fear. It worked as an emetic to the emotions through what we call "catharsis."[32] He was capturing the intensity of art made possible precisely by the fact that we are not asked to get involved in solving the problems of the characters. All of our energy is channeled into watching, not acting.

3.4121 For this reason we can only say what art is by seeing how people react to specific objects. There need be no final unanimity about what art is, but there are likely to be some areas of very strong overlap.

3.42 For many people, watching sports function like the arts. There are winners and losers, and neither of them is us. There is drama in the form of suspense and abrupt reverses.

3.421 The advantage of sports is that it is real, in a way that a tragedy is not. Somebody really wins the game.

We don't know how it will turn out, either: it is like a play being made up before us. Before the game is played, there is no winner.

The disadvantage of sports is that the stakes are fairly small. All people do is win a game, not live or die.

3.4211 Sports that posed a real threat to the participants, such as Roman gladiatorial combat or the pre-Columbian American ball-game, had to be carried out between people clearly of a different group than the spectators. Otherwise these would function not as sports, but as real-life threats.

3.43 We personally may be unconcerned with mudslides in a part of the world we are uninterested in, and we report the tragedies of history with great equanimity. But someone may well be upset about these things. They will be a part of somebody's projects.

The only way to guarantee that we remain off the pathways of people's projects is to make the people fictional, so that no matter how many planes we take, we will not find them when we get off.

3.44 Thinkers from Plato to John Searle have failed to see that being fictional is a real quality based on the location of people and events with respect to our projects, not merely a lack of being real.[33]

Fictional characters are precisely the kind of character that exists in the body of the world ignored by our projects.

This too is part of reality. It is the largest part of reality.

3.5 Art avoids the obvious.

3.51 The world is shot through with obvious things. They are things we all know because they are part of commonly undertaken projects. In order to be able to avoid the obvious, art must be aware of the obvious, or at least of avoiding it.

3.511 Most of what people say is predictable: we can see well-worn analogies coming, see obvious jokes, that astonishingly the people go ahead and make.

To the people themselves, they do not seem predictable, because they are appropriate to the circumstances in which they are used. They solve specific problems.

The only reason we may smile in pity is that the person clearly thinks he or she is being interesting, not because in fact there is no surprise in what he or she does.

3.512 Most body gestures are quite banal. It is always appropriate to shake hands, to stand still, to lean forward to express interest. People aren't trying to be interesting, they are trying to do the thing that is appropriate for this particular situation.

Unless that very predictability is the point and is underscored by relentless repetition, a dance—the art form of gesture and body movement—will be unable to use them. Even then, we see them from the outside, not be within them: a dance that incorporates the motions of people greeting is about people seeming to greet, not people actually greeting.

3.5121 Saying that the world is predictable is like being bored by rooms and rooms full of eighteenth-century English portraits, or dozens of fourteenth-century Madonnas. They only overwhelm us because there are so many of them here at once, taken out of the drawing rooms of the country houses and the apses of the churches where each once hung alone.

3.513 As an analogy to the way art avoids the obvious, there is the fact that some of the positions of the hands on an analog watch face are more aesthetically pleasing than others. Those with no aesthetic value are the obvious positions, the ones that are most usual divisions of a circle. The quarters are uninteresting (12:00, 3:00 and so on), positions that fail to fill the face are uninteresting (6:30). We can move minute-by-minute around the clock face, saying which minutes are more interesting than others and why: in some cases we feel them being dragged by the approaching quarters or halves; in other cases we sense them leaving these strong "magnet points." The more interesting positions, those with some aesthetic grace, will be those like 8:07 or perhaps 4:51, where the arms fill most of the face but are not on the "obvious" positions, nor too obviously avoiding them.

3.514 It's usually easier to say when the artist has succeeded in avoiding the obvious (when the art "works") than what the obvious is that s/he is avoiding. We can say whether the artwork is good or bad, but not necessarily why. For this, the trained eye of the critic may be useful.

3.52 It's possible to avoid the obvious in many aspects of the world. The result is differing kinds and forms of art. Words and plots can be made interesting to produce novels. Avoiding obvious movement can lead to interesting dances.

If the avoidance is so great we no longer sense what's being avoided, we are simply lost in the thicket and the artwork has no meaning. It's no longer an avoidance of an obvious point, just part of the much larger world that has no structuring at all.

3.521 It would take a particular set of circumstances for us to see as interesting the movements of a group of people really getting up from the restaurant table next to ours, rather than on stage. We might be on the other side of a pane of glass, and so abruptly see them in mute dumb-show. Not understanding what they say could make the silent motions interesting.

3.522 The techniques of art, its frames, are what give us this outside perspective. The frames of a dance include the fact that it is on a stage, we don't know the people we see, they bow at the end, we have paid to be there, and it all starts at a specific time.

3.523 One of these techniques is imitation, which is thus only a means to an end, and not the *sine qua non* of art that Aristotle, in the *Poetics*, thought it was.

Imitation works like the pane of glass. We see what's on the other side.

Not all art involves imitation. Think of Duchamps's urinal and bottle-rack "ready-mades."[34]

3.53 The Russian Formalist Victor Shklovsky, in his essay "Art as Technique," quoted from Tolstoy's diary saying that when he, Tolstoy, went to dust the furniture, he couldn't remember if he'd done so or not.[35] Shklovsky's horrified response was that this meant that life was as if it had never been. Awareness of life, for Shklovsky, was the same as experiencing it.

3.531 Realizing that most of life passes us by when we are not aware of it, Shklovsky concluded that only artists could give us back the world. They make us aware of it: "art makes the stone stony," he insisted.[36] Without art, the world has no taste. And so it has failed to be.

3.5311 Artists can make us aware of the world, but it is not true to say that only they can do so. We can be aware of the world by means of many things, of which artists are only one. Another is, simply sitting still for a moment and looking around.

3.5312 Shklovsky was right that artists can help us to become aware of the world we're unaware of being unaware of since typically artists are not climbing the same corporate ladder of the most of the rest of us and so see different things. Or they see what we see, but differently. They can show us what our paths look like to someone on the outside.

The Formalists thought this was the nature of all art, and called it "making strange." This is neither a necessary nor sufficient condition for something to be art.

3.532 We can be spectators of the dance of life by sitting on the sidelines in a major airport's International Arrivals Hall for an hour.

3.5321 We can enjoy these things without artists, but if we are not an artist, we are unlikely to be able to transmit the reason for our enjoyment to others. This is the only thing art is good for: not for making us see these things, but for making others do so.

3.5322 Not everyone wants to transmit this enjoyment to others. Those that do attempt to do this become artists.

3.5323 Through their works, artists set up situations where these things can be enjoyed with some degree of predictability. We go to the theater or to an art gallery in hopes of being more interested in what we see than by staying at home.

3.533 Artworks increase the probability, with respect to a randomly selected equivalent amount of the rest of life, of our having an experience of interest, but they do not guarantee it.

3.5331 What is interesting for us may be boring for our neighbor. Frequently some critics love X, some hate it.

3.5332 Students may remain resoundingly indifferent to works that the professor thinks should move them profoundly. This frustrates professors.

3.534 Artworks are works where we do have such an experience. (This is why Kant was going about things backwards, and why ultimately he is a fascist. Anybody who believes he has solved all problems for all time is a fascist. Part of Wittgenstein's personality was sympathetic to this point of view. What makes him interesting as a thinker is that he was a self-destructive fascist. These are rare.)

3.535 Those who go to an art museum thinking they are guaranteed to have this experience are simply misguided.

We should go to an art gallery the way we may go to a party full of new people. We know they will be new people, we know they will probably be trying to make a good impression, but we cannot guarantee we will find everyone interesting, or even most people. We go to find something interesting, not everything.

3.536 We may ask, is object X art?

The people most concerned with defining an artwork from what is not an artwork are those who run museums, write syllabi for colleges: what to choose, what to leave out? Their concerns need not determine ours.

3.5361 Such people frequently feel they are defending the honor of art, or of artworks.

Art has no honor to defend. Syllabi and museums are transient things, not lists or storehouses of Greatest Works of All Time.

That's why getting something in a museum or on a syllabus is really quite a trivial thing, in artistic terms. In terms of curatorial self-interest or financial advantage to the artist, it can be quite an important thing.

3.537 An object before us may be an artwork for you and not for me, or the reverse. Art is a situation, not an object, though we may find ourselves in the situation as a result of the object.

Trying to define art by classifying objects is the downfall of the aesthetic theory of the last century. Modernism starts with the focus on the object.

5.538 Instead we should say: an artwork is a situation where someone intended us to have a certain kind of experience. We can only say after the experience, therefore, whether the object was an artwork or something else. The world is full of something elses.

3.5381 We can have this experience of interest without the artist, say on the beach all alone, watching the birds, but it was not intended. We do not need the artist to have this experience; we only need the artist to have art.

3.5382 This is one experience: The view out of an anteroom with a coffee maker containing a few inches of tepid coffee, stumbled into next to the gift shop of the temporary quarters of a museum. Then, looking up: out the wide window, in the distance, the skyscrapers of Manhattan shrouded in fog. In front, an elevated parking lot with the repeated shapes and colors of parked yellow taxi cabs. Down below, at street level, the concave cups of a spooning row of the yellow hoods of other cabs, like painted finger nails neatly arranged in a horizontal pile. Off to the left, the curving letters of a business floating on a grid above the roof of the low building. Off to the right, the crinkled surfaces of plastic strung over a row of windows revealed down the rooftop corridor of a building below eye level. And in the center, on the window in front of our eyes, a spinning exhaust fan, a tiny moving circle around which this so-complex world seems to turn, moving air from nowhere to nowhere, bereft of its inside and outside.

Or: on the way to this spot, the white insides of a building under renovation gushing dusty shattered innards of chalk onto the street, while men with power tools and covered in white dust move about inside like the spirits of the ghostly building.

3.5383 These are far more interesting than most artworks.

Perhaps this is what Kant meant when he said that we sense beauty when we perceive nature as if it had been intended: it looks like an artwork, only we know there's no artist.

This is backwards. Nature isn't a flawed artwork. Artworks are the attempt to guarantee the experience of interest that occurs naturally, though unpredictably.

3.539 Some people, misled as Shklovsky was misled, think they are saving the human race from boredom if they figure out how to offer these things these things to other people. An installation, complete with dust and broken rocks? Perhaps even including the power tool man, if he can be induced to stand in the museum all day?

3.5391 Contemporary art is about this: signing the world and proclaiming it an artwork. But by what right can I appropriate such great swaths of the world and offer them to others? They don't belong to me in the first place.

3.5392 Contemporary art is full of works produced by people who thought they had to present the world to us. They don't.

3.5393 The artist asks this: How do I transmit the view from the window? Perhaps through a photograph? This wouldn't be ideal, as that would eliminate the motion of the tiny fan in the center, so seminal to this experience. A video? Are there video frames wide enough to capture the full side to side, the up and down? And will this moment ever come again? While I am running for my video camera, or even fumbling in my case (if I have thought to bring it), the moment is gone forever.

3.5394 How insulting to go to a museum and find things that are creaky, school-marmy "look at this, class!" versions of what we find tenfold on the street every day with no schoolmarm and no coercion, assuming we keep our eyes open! Do so-called artists really think we are so helpless as to need them to notice these things? And how dull are the things in museum, precisely because they are in museums. When we stumble over them by chance they hit us like bolts of lightning; when we go expecting to be surprised we usually aren't. The very act of offering this thing as art vitiates much late twentieth-century and early twenty-first-century visual art, because the viewer's expectations are so much higher for so much less.

Many museums of contemporary art spoon-feed us pablum, as if we are not capable of getting ourselves real food all by ourselves.

3.5395 The techniques of art are facts in the world, and so can become ends in themselves. We think operas are things that look a certain way, and so we make yet another opera, defined as something that looks like this. Such a view of techniques as providing the definition for art produces "academic" art, such as painting in the nineteenth century, or perhaps the interminable soft-headed "this quirky little thing happened to me" lyric poetry in ours. Good works of art have something they transmit; the technique is secondary.

3.54 Some people have confused art's avoidance of the obvious with its being less than serious. We don't have to pay attention to it to get our work done. Of course this is true, but that is true of most of life as well that we are simply unaware of.

Art functions in the area of the world we were unaware of (but not too far off the beaten paths).

3.541 For those concentrating on the functional, and whose projects are largely set by others, art seems merely frippery: it's not part of moving forward.

3.542 It is always true that what individual X is not using for his or her projects is not, to that person, "functional." But it may be functional when that person's projects change, or for another person. It is the raw material of all functionality.

Communication

3.6 Art is not communication, say between an author and a viewer or reader. Many thinkers have held that it is.

3.61 An act of communication always has two parts. We may call these parts the question (though it may not be in the form of a question) and a response.

For communication to occur, we have to react to what we are told or see in some way the person trying to communicate with us understands to be a response. We can grunt, or nod, or merely do what is asked of us. Sometimes years go by before the questioner is able to say that communication has taken place: finally someone answers our letter or e-mail. Someone tells us that we were right, lo those many years ago. Or, for that matter, wrong.

3.611 We can say when communication has taken place, but we can only guess that it has not taken place.

3.612 The more formulaic the response we expect, the more social the interaction.

We are sure communication has taken place if we say, or the other person says, "I see," or "yes," or grunt, or when we say what the circumstances require, such as "I do" during a marriage ceremony.

Signing our name functions in this same way. In itself, it is an arbitrary action. But when we do it, it has certain meanings. We sign, or don't sign: our choices seem limited to two.

3.613 The philosopher John Searle was very interested in these formulaic responses.[37] He thought they were odd ducks in the world, and called them "performatives." He thought they somehow made things happen.

They don't. The illusion that they do is produced by our having narrowed the range of awaited responses to the question. It's the narrowness of possible responses, which we've created, that makes this illusion.

Besides, we never guarantee that the only possible responses are two, doing X or not doing X. We say they are, and believe that we have thereby made them so.

3.614 All social interactions will be somewhat formulaic. Our responses are limited, but they're not as limited as they seem to be when it appears our options are signing or not signing.

If someone asks us for a match on the street, we can give him/her one, or say we don't smoke. We probably won't recite the Gettysburg Address. But we could. What does this mean? We don't know. (Most of the world is off the paths of the expected, so far off as to be meaningless.)

Performatives are the case of greatest limitation, where the only meaning we allow hinges on either saying or not saying one specific thing. People are waiting for us to do this one thing, and when we do, everyone applauds. We have done it! No wonder Searle thought that words were actually making the world come to be. But that's only because the expected response was so expected. That's all people were waiting for.

But instead of saying "I do," or "I pronounce you man and wife," we can begin to laugh hysterically, or whistle "Dixie." Or perhaps say "I do" and then laugh hysterically, and whistle "Dixie." Where is the performative now? Has the marriage happened or not? It's not the words that change the world, it's the fact that people accept them as changing the world that changes the world.

What we don't accept doesn't change the world. In making strange responses, we've gotten off the path defined by perfect prediction.

3.615 Performatives are what seem (but aren't) completely social situations. (We can always personalize them.)

In more personal situations, the response is allowed to define the question retroactively to some degree: the rigidity of performatives is abandoned. Responses aren't merely binary.

3.6151 If "How are you?" *must* elicit "fine" as a response, the interaction is completely social. If "How are you?" could lead to an answer about our head cold or our sick dog, the interaction is more personal.

3.62 In artworks, the question and its response are made for each other. They form a closed unit. The response is a response to this question only. It is perfectly particular.

For this reason we, the perceiver, do not have to respond to the object in front of us. It's already taken care of both halves of the communication situation.

3.621 Of course, someone may be standing over us telling us how to respond. "Class, what do you think of the main character?" And we must respond.

3.622 This is a communication situation, but it is not communication with the work. It is communication with the teacher.

We can strip away this communication situation, and with it disappears the constraints of the social situation. We have freedom of response. No one is checking up on us.

3.63 This is the freedom offered by art.

It can give us the same flat frieze effect of childhood: it merely is. Part of what it merely is can be pleas to action, but these work like the tantrums of celebrities: they are part of the show. We look impassively even at this. Or not, as we choose. No one tells us we have to; if we do, it's because we choose to.

3.631 Art offers glides on the ice as opposed to the friction of most of life.

3.632 Because art is excerpts from worlds that are not part of our action patterns, it gives us a sense of the richness of the world. It gives us a vacation.

Because we choose it, rather than it us, it can sometimes offer a better vacation than a place with a pool and servants.

Emily Dickinson said, "There is no frigate like a book/ to take us lands away."[38] She may have meant that the respite provided by art is absolute, whereas when we are geographically, lands away, we still have to pay the bill, or fend off intruders, go to the bathroom, and get our sleep. We may have to do these things before, during, or after perceiving an artwork, but we compartmentalize these things, close them out. They are not part of the experience.

3.633 Artworks are the domesticated exotic. Their initial pull is less because they are right here under our nose. Yet we do not have to get on a frigate, or plane, to taste their worlds.

3.634 Works are not guaranteed to give us an experience of interest. But when they do, it is an experience that does not dissipate, the way the aura of the exotic does when we go to the exotic place.

3.635 Those who dismiss art believe that it is possible to achieve both reality and intensity.

3.6351 In fact, we always have a choice: intensity *or* reality. We cannot have both.

We can be focused on the path, or off it, either moving forward or enjoying the sense of a diorama moving by us.

3.6352 Each of us uses up his or her personal exotics.

3.63521 This leads to the sad plight of Tennyson's Ulysses in the poem bearing his name.[39]

Ulysses is come home from the Trojan Wars and his Odyssey but longs for new adventures. "I cannot rest from travel," he says. He finds his loyal wife, Penelope, old; his son Telemachus seems too prim for his taste, and his people are a "savage race." All he wants to do is leave again on another adventure. Called to rule, all he can think is this: "There lies the port; the vessel puffs her sail." Once at sea again, he may drown, or not. He knows that both are options. All he wants is to leave, though he knows that the goal is the voyage itself. He will never get what he is aiming at, for he is pushed eternally onwards. "All experience is an arch wherethrough/ Gleams that untravelled world whose margin fades/ forever and forever when I move."

We can make the unknown world part of our projects in the search for the real exotic. But this always changes the nature of the exotic into something attained, part of the reality of our project, something we have mastered.

3.64 We can't master art in general, because part of each artwork is situated just off the patterns of our projects.

If it is too far off, it is simply meaningless. There is more space in which it can be meaningless than in which it can be meaningful.

Sometimes we can't tell if the work is meaningless only because it diverges too far from our own personal projects, or because it diverges too far from the societal obvious.

3.641 If we do master specific works, as an art history professor has done who leads us through a gallery, talking and scarcely looking right or left, they have ceased, for him or her, to be art.

3.642 We use up art, the way we use up the exotic. But there is always more art, as there may not always be undiscovered corners of the world to put a hotel in.

There is always more art because there is always undiscovered something, even if it is the pattern of shiny asphalt patchings on the roadway, a tiny drama of a street encounter that we watch from a café.

3.643 When art has gone a certain distance in one direction, it simply reverses course: the over-refined work of the nineteenth century gave way to a taste for the "primitive." And this in turn to other tastes.

The more completely we mine a vein the more certain it is that ultimately people will want other veins. We only mine out one vein, not all, because the others have to be discovered.

3.65 People who make art locate it just beyond our grasp.

3.66 Art works like a time bomb. We leave a book for decades on our shelf, and then are shattered when finally we taken it down and open it.

We can walk by the library building all our lives. Or we can enter.

3.67 Those who think they can make art part of their projects have never tried to look at the stars: the sides of the eyes are the more receptive to seeing such things. In order to perceive the stars, we must look away from them, not directly at them.

3.68 We cannot storm the halls of art. The door gives way to reveal a vast emptiness. But if we look down quietly at our feet, there it is, waiting for us.

How do we relate to others in the social world?

4 The personal world is different from the social world. This difference is produced by the relative positions of both, not by their intrinsic nature.

4.01 The social world is defined as situations that require us in turn to act in certain ways. It is formulaic. The personal world lacks these constraints. We make it up as we go along. Usually the social world involves other people, but it need not: the proverbial Victorian Englishman on his island faithfully dressing for dinner is following social rules, even if he is surrounded by people who don't follow those rules. For him, this is simply the way to do it.

The conversation with the woman behind the cash register at the store is likely to be almost completely formulaic, social. There are only a few things we can legitimately say. Usually we say nothing at all; we stand and wait until she is finished. Perhaps we smile. But if we were to discover that she baby-sat us when we were a child, we would suddenly have many more (personal) things to say that are not codified by the nature of the engagement.

4.02 Personal and social are relative to each other, not absolute. Whichever is more codified is the more social. At the ends of the spectrum, there are some interactions that are completely social at one end, or completely personal at the other. (See 3.615.)

4.03 Personal and social are the expression in terms of other people of the distinction between our projects and the uncharted world they both organize and ignore.

4.04 Personal is correlated to some degree to solitary, but it is not identical with it.

4.041 Many of our projects are determined by others. Many of our goals are social.

4.042 I can be alone and still be pursuing a goal. But the chances are greater I will be able to be aware of the things around me that are irrelevant to that goal if I don't have to interact with someone else. (See 2.01.)

4.043 Some of the time spent away from projects can be shared. We can enjoy a vacation with someone else, or climb a mountain with that person.

4.05 If we wish to really strike out across the brush as part of our project, it is usually easier to do it alone. If we are very lucky, we can do it with someone with whom we have a personal relationship. Such a person knows the value of silence.

4.051 A developed sexual relationship almost always strikes out across the brush with one other person. It makes itself up as it goes along.

4.06 We may speak of the "personal world" as if it were a place. In fact it is really only a succession of moments of varying length and intensity.

4.061 Thinking that the personal world exists in absolute contrast to the social leads to philosophical dualism such as Descartes', only possible for someone who did spend a great deal of time alone. Descartes was sure of his own existence, but doubted that of other people.[40]

Other dualists have included the Modernists: Virginia Woolf, James Joyce, E. M. Forster. For them, the social world was a lie; only the personal world was real.

4.1 When we enter the personal world, for whatever length of time and however absolutely, the world regains to that degree the solidity it had in childhood.

I'm free to marvel at the profusion of the world, rather than eliminating it to serve my own purposes.

I don't try to control it. In exchange for not controlling it, it opens itself to me.

4.11 I stand alone in an exhibit of photographs of cityscapes, transfixed at the way the highly polished gray floors with the interrupted trapezoids of light entering from doorways reflected blurred versions of the pictures on the walls, as if the world did not end at the floor but only continued downward, and myself suspended at half-height within it. A few minutes later, I look out the window at the transitory patterns of the spume of water in the central courtyard that reaches to the top story of the museum, where I stand equal to or slightly above its apogee, as if seeing it frozen in mid-air. There is a rainbow at the water's base, probably invisible from the ground. As I watch, a little girl, miniaturized by distance, moves ahead of her mother and begins to run, then falls. I watch the mother pick the child up in small-sized dumb-show, dust her off, comfort her, and set her on her feet again. She darts forward and is lost under the building.

These people didn't know I watched them, or that I smiled at the thought that such moments occur billions of unremarked times all around us every day. I could merely watch, or smile, as I choose: no one cares.

4.111 No one caring is the hallmark of the personal world. This means, our interaction is not codified. In this case, given that I was three floors up and behind glass, no interaction was possible.

4.112 The personal world is scary to some people: nobody is giving us approbation. Indeed no one else knows it exists. But I do.

4.113 If my knowledge that it exists isn't good enough, I can try to share it. But everyone else has his or her comparable world, and it's not clear they want to share mine. Or that mine is worth sharing. And how is it made better if someone else is aware of it? Then it's only part of their personal world too. Do we both then have to share it with a third person, and a fourth, and so on?

4.114 If the personal world is meaningless, most of the world is meaningless.

Knowledge

4.2 Knowledge forms a spectrum.

There are different kinds of knowledge in the world.

4.21 The largest bulk of our knowledge is about and located in our personal worlds. It is knowledge on which we are never tested and that is used up in the moment. Personal knowledge is wedded to the situation that created it, and evaporates when this situation changes. We may call this "situational knowledge."

At the other end of the spectrum is scientific knowledge, which aspires to be independent of situations.

In between are codified practical knowledge we call "skills," also the codified knowledge about specialized facets of the world we call "disciplines," also the generalized knowledge of the world we call "wisdom."

Science

4.22 Science is a specific undertaking, it is not the prototype of all knowledge.

Scientific knowledge is one kind of knowledge. It gets its nature from being an alternative to other kinds of knowledge.

4.23 For personal knowledge, "knowing that" is the same as "knowing how," a distinction made by the philosopher Gilbert Ryle.[41] Because our knowledge is practical, it is used up in the moment.

4.231 This is what personal knowledge looks like: I am sitting at a corner, waiting to pull into traffic. I watch both directions, my foot on the brake. I look to the right: I can't go. There are three cars in a row, and I can't see past the curve. I check out the left: empty, but by the time the three cars on the right go by, there are an SUV and a minivan barreling my way. I kept looking to the right, where two cars are on their way, and by this time there is a whole red light's worth of traffic coming from the left. I let my eyes blur, uncrick my neck, and in a few seconds check again. I think I see a hole opening up: if the red car on the right stays back a certain amount I can get in before the ones on the left. It happens! I see the hole I need, and I pull into traffic. That was the moment when I could pull into traffic.

Knowing that I could pull into traffic at this point is knowledge. But it is momentary knowledge, used up in the instant of its application. No one else is interested in the fact that on this day, in this pattern of cars, I could pull into traffic at this point. This is almost totally "knowing that."

Personal knowledge

4.3 A good deal of situational knowledge doesn't initially seem to be knowledge at all, because we are unaware of possessing it.

Nothing is requiring us to think about it. We aren't aware of having worked for it, and nobody else is expressing an interest in it.

We know a million things just to put our socks on in the morning, starting with where the socks are. Yet usually we don't know we know, and in any case don't share that knowledge with anyone. If we do become aware of them, they suddenly seem substantial.

4.31 Becoming aware of them can be the first step to sharing them, which makes them public rather than private knowledge, or the first step of transforming them into other sorts of knowledge.

4.32 Becoming aware of the vast realm of situational knowledge causes the relationship between foreground and background to change in our perception of the world, the way we can suddenly become aware of all the sounds we unconsciously block out.

4.34 The personal world isn't a content of knowledge, but a placement. What is in the personal world can become public.

Recently my mother-in-law and her husband got lost driving to our new house. They had made it to the main north-south street nearby, but turned north on it rather than south. I figured this out when Klaus called me, saying they were turning in circles. "What do you see?" I asked. He named some street names, and then began naming the stores. Suddenly I knew where they were. I talked them to our house. I knew how to do this, I realized.

Who would have said that a visual imprint of the road I drive twice daily could be useful information to anyone? It suddenly took on value when another person wanted it. Almost everyone in the two mile radius around me could probably have done the same thing, but my mother-in-law had no means of contacting them. For her purposes, I was the only one who had this information.

Similarly, we get scientists to talk to us about science because they are the only ones we know with this information. All the inhabitants of some distant galaxy may know what only five Nobel Prize winners on Earth know, but we do not have access to them.

4.341 Whether or not we say we "know" something depends on the vagaries of the market—whether somebody else wants to know what we know or not. If they do, not only does what we know suddenly acquire value, it becomes something to be known. That is, it is something that was known.

4.342 Everyone has experiences like this, situational knowledge that enters the social world and so comes to light. Occasionally, some of the things of which our private worlds are composed have greatness thrust upon 'em. Suddenly we find ourselves in court, with an army of lawyers focusing on the minutest details of a day we had completely forgotten. Who knew that someday someone would be interested in this? Or one day a family member asks us about a departed person, or a television crew arrives to interview us as the Last Living Whatever and demands our recollections. Suddenly, we might say, somebody cares. Or alternately, for whatever reason we are suddenly willing to share things that we have kept for ourselves for decades.

The private realm is the ocean on which float the islands of the social.

4.343 Molière's M. Jordan made the delighted discovery that he spoke "prose."[42] This is funny precisely because it is similar to the way most of us are unaware of what we know. With personal knowledge, we don't usually know that we know something until we need it for something. Sometimes, we don't know what we've learned until we come to teach it to someone.

4.344 Most of our knowledge of people is personal knowledge. There is nothing scientific about it. Frequently it cannot be confirmed and the situation isn't repeatable.

William Hazlitt gives the example of a man visiting in the house of a woman who, he notes, is treating her daughter with an abnormal degree of respect.[43] The visitor concludes that the daughter has married the Duke with whom she had been coupled in conversation. His evidence is merely the respect of the mother. A few days later he hears of the marriage, and is vindicated.

Unlike science, this is the real world. He could not force disclosure of the information. He cannot treat life as if it were a laboratory, where we have unlimited access to the data, and can assume that what we're studying will be there in the morning. Perhaps his social class precludes his asking what happened, and in any case the woman's daughter might well have denied everything.

Science is about forcing disclosure by the world. This only works under those circumstances when we are dealing with that small part of the world that can be forced, and where the fact of the scientist plays no role.

4.3441 Most things in the world are unknowable in this sense, for purely practical reasons. Yet practical reasons compose most of life.

Why did a certain former girlfriend break up with me? I may have my theories, but she may well deny them out of pique, or refuse to speak to me altogether if I called her up now after so many years to ask.

There are many options other than telling sober, objective truth.

4.3442 Very few things in the world are free of the situational constraints that make treating them in a scientific way impossible. This is why science has to take place outside of the run of normal life, and usually uses other vocabulary than the vocabulary of normal life.

4.3443 Freud attempted to render the human being scientific. Thus he had to assume unlimited access and repeatability. If the person involved denied him access, he had to explain this in scientific terms.

There are many reasons why someone talking about his or her innermost thoughts might say X or Y was not so, the least important of them being that X or Y was not the case. Most evident is unwillingness to speak these things to another person, much less to a bully as Freud apparently was.

4.3444 We sometimes speak of our "messy" humanity, the fact that people are shades of gray rather than black and white, and shot through with contradictions. But people are only messy compared with something they have created, namely science. This is like saying that human love is messy because it is not the eternal love of the people on Keats's urn.[44] We were the ones who made the urn to begin with, as an ideal. Of course we can never attain it. Attaining it wasn't the point. Dreaming about it was.

There is nothing particularly messy about humanity. To see this we have only to understand that lack of knowledge is the Janus face of all knowledge, the iceberg under the tiny hard tip we emphasize. Humanity is what it is.

4.35 Some things about ourselves are beyond our knowledge. We come to realize them with time. At any given time, we would deny that X was so, and suddenly one day relent and say it was, merely because until that point it had not seemed to us that X was the case.

We did not need Freud to realize this, though he gave names to the mechanisms by which we do this. He carved the roads so that it seems self-evident to reach for expressions like "repression" rather than making us bushwhack and justify them each time.

Skills

4.4 We codify knowledge that only a small group of people have to know and call it technical knowledge, or skills. The rest of us go to these specialists to have our problems taken care of.

4.41 It's already knowledge to know if something falls into this codified category, or if we have to do it ourselves as best we can.

It is just as much "knowing" to know whom to call as to know how to deal with it yourself. It was knowledge I didn't have to know to look in the yellow pages under "Trappers." (See 1.11.) That solved my problem.

4.411 Romantics, like Marx, resist dependency on others implied by specialization.[45] But even in Marx's pre-industrial world, the individual didn't make his own plows or horse collars. There was a specialist for each of these things.

4.412 We can sympathize with Marx's fear of loss of control that dependence on others probably implied to him. But we feel no loss of control when we know whom to call. Yet we still depend on others.

Change is what takes control from us, not the intrinsic circumstances. We remember things in our grasp; now they are not. Our children, who grew up with these things, will not feel out of control, but very much in control: they know exactly whom to call, or how to work the newest gadget.

4.42 Skills are mutable. They are social, but with short half-lives. What counts as a skill is only what people say counts as a skill.

A Baltimore radio station runs ads for a computer school by pointing out that if you trained as a TV repairman in the 60s or 70s, you might think you were set with a job for life. TV repairmen, it points out, aren't very sought after nowadays. (They want you to train as a computer specialist.)

This means that you never know when things you learned how to do will come in handy. Suddenly knowledge that seemed only disposable knowledge is useful in other circumstances.

4.43 Skills are a bit closer to science than personal knowledge.

We may be able to articulate scientific principles behind (say) changing the oil on the car. Because they are codified and generally disseminated, we can name some: the pressure of the screw that holds on the filter, the gravity that allows the oil to flow out into the pan, and so on. But we don't discover these things from changing the oil, and they are irrelevant to the action of changing it.

Nor is there any pretense to eternal status of such rules as we have: turn the filter hard, put the pan right under the hole, etc. One day car filters may be different. One day we may no longer have cars. They are life skills, useful to us, but not at the highest level of generality.

4.5 The person who changes my oil changes the oil of every car that comes in; the person who cuts my hair cuts the hair of everyone who has an appointment. Aside from an initial learning situation, there is little interaction between practitioners: the vector arrow in each case is back to the undifferentiated social world.

When skills lose some degree of their "knowing how" and separate more from the world of utility into a world of "knowing that," they form developed sub-worlds of knowledge. We call these "disciplines." They are marked by extensive interaction between their practitioners, all working together on the knowledge that for the rest of the world remains esoteric. (Knowledge of how to cut hair may be specialized, but it is used up to a greater degree through the act of cutting hair.)

Disciplines are limited social worlds.

4.51 Disciplines link back to the world as a whole: we study Art History, or the Maya. It is not used up in the act of transmitting some of its bulk, in the way that the skill of hair cutting is used up in its application.

4.52 I can write books about the Maya, or Rembrandt. I do so largely for the other people in my discipline, or for those times when the discipline as a whole contacts the world outside. The reason I don't write books about the problems I had trying to get grass to grow on my backyard is that no one but me is interested in the grass.

The grass in my back yard is not a discipline. It has not been made one.

If no one but me is interested in Rembrandt or the Maya, the knowledge I get of the paintings or the writing system of the Maya is private.

4.53 People are engaged in disciplines collectively. What makes them disciplines is that other people than myself are involved in them.

4.6 More general than skills or disciplines is knowledge that is expressible as a generalization of precise situations. This is wisdom.

Wisdom

4.61 Skills and disciplines are defined by their practice by either individuals or groups of people. Wisdom is a solitary form of knowledge. It is the generalization of situational knowledge, not a sub-group of general knowledge.

4.62 Wisdom is not verifiable. If we say, children are different than adults, or teenagers are mopey, it may be that some aspect of this can be put into scientific terms: certain hormones lead to behaviors observed in 77% of test subjects etc. But wisdom has a greater situational link than science, is more tied to things as they are right now.

4.63 Wisdom has a great admixture of "knowing how." We show wisdom by acting wisely, saying the right thing, doing the right thing. We merely sigh, clean up after the two-year-old, perhaps tell him "no" in terms we think will be accessible to him, and go on with our lives. If our teen-agers are rebellious, we do not rail at them, but let them know we love them and are there to guide them.

4.64 Wisdom, when it is codified, frequently becomes platitudes, because it is so linked to a great number of situations.

4.65 It is almost impossible to teach wisdom. Wisdom must be learned. We can build up to it, construct it. Because it is constructed, its link with life as lived is too situational. The construction cannot be linked to others' lives.

4.651 People can try to teach us wisdom without our learning it. Because wisdom is linked to the world, we have to see the connection between the flower of wisdom and the ground in which it grew. If people cut it and hand it to us, we typically don't know what to do with it. It seems strange, perhaps beautiful, but alien.

4.652 The impossibility of teaching wisdom is one of the great tragic facts of life. Wisdom costs us so much, and turns out to have no value for anyone but ourselves. What a waste, we think.

4.6521 This is first cousin to the feelings of melancholy when we look at faded photographs of long-dead athletes. It seems unspeakable that these clear-eyed boys should have become old and withered, and are now rottenness, have returned to earth.

4.6522 But there is more youth where that came from, and more bodies. Their youthful bodies were for themselves alone, not for us. Why pity them?

4.6523 The impossibility of teaching wisdom usually becomes clear to us at the same time we are aware of another of the great tragic facts of life, that our children, who seem so intimate to us, are in other ways complete strangers. (See 2.931.) These things dawn on us when we are trying to teach wisdom to our children.

4.6524 We can't force wisdom on someone who doesn't want it. This is called the teaching posture: Listen To Me!

Instead we must wait until others ask us for what we know. This is called the learning posture: Teach Me! (See 1.53.)

4.66 The arts are the form in which much wisdom is expressed, though not necessarily passed on. This is so because we can only approach the arts in the learning posture. They cannot be taught either. But we can learn from them.

4.661 The arts allow situations which are precise enough for the expression of the wisdom, but not so precise that they become disposable knowledge, not so general that they are separated from circumstances in the form of scientific pronouncements. Think of the great truths in E. B. White's *Charlotte's Web*, the story of a spider who teaches a pig about the beauty and brevity of life.[46] This is certainly wisdom too deep for tears, though many of us weep at precisely this fact.

Belief

4.7 Another form of knowledge, belief, is defined by its relationship to the collective. It is in a sense the inverse of disciplines, which are understood as sub-groups within a larger whole. Belief systems are built so as to escape control by the larger whole.

4.71 Religion and nationality are major sources of belief systems.

Members of religion X believe that they will (say) fry in hell if they do Y or Z. For members of religion Y it is A or B that may not be done. Patriotism is a belief system: it asks everyone within the bounds of a certain geographical entity (country, state, region) to believe certain things, say the superiority of Americans, or Frenchmen. This is not based on proof; the belief is the end of the road. The point is getting there, not how you do it.

4.72 All religions seem strange to those outside of them. For those not brought up on the story of Christianity, tales of a virgin birth and a God bleeding on a cross seem bizarre. For those not brought up on Islam, stories of a night journey, with the Prophet flying through the air, seem equally bizarre. Christians laugh that a hair of the Prophet's beard is held worth cherishing in Islam, but do not blink an eye at claims for the Shroud of Turin. Or if they doubt relics in each case, they nonetheless hold that the Son of God really suffered under Pontius Pilate, was crucified, died, and was buried. All monotheisms are aghast at the proliferation of gods in polytheisms. What could be more ridiculous than a god with the head of an elephant! Yet Ganesh is one of the most revered gods of all Hinduism.

4.73 Lack of proof is not what distinguishes religious or patriotic beliefs from other beliefs. Most beliefs are never subjected to the demand for proof, and we would be unable to prove those that are. They not only lack proof, we've never even tried to look for it.

4.731 There is nothing intrinsically fragile about belief, and questioning beliefs is not the proof of their strength. Our lives are successfully undergirded by beliefs that are never questioned. I believe that water will quench my thirst. I believe that the floor I walk on will support my weight. I believe that friend X is a good person.

Unquestioned beliefs are part of the water holding up our boat. We don't have to question them to have the boat float. The boat floats anyway.

We can do without any specific belief, but we cannot do without all beliefs. And most beliefs are never questioned.

Questioning beliefs is typically their death knell. The strongest beliefs are those that aren't questioned.

Beliefs are like fairies: if you leave them alone, they are (some people say) all around you. If you try to catch them or root them out, they fly away.

4.74 Belief systems are different from most beliefs in that they are publicly codified beliefs. They teach people what to believe. Many of them include credos. When people recite a credo, they know what they believe, because that is exactly what they are saying. *Credo* means "I believe." That way they can answer the question, "What do you believe?"

4.75 The nature of belief systems is the shared, codified nature of the belief. The demand for proof of such beliefs by definition cuts away the basis of belief systems, their shared nature. It announces that the person making this demand is not a member of this belief system.

4.76 Belief systems by their nature cannot be proven. They are for this reason not scientific. Not being scientific, however, is a quality of all sorts of knowledge other than science, so this is not particularly noteworthy.

4.761 Unverifiable is the best option for religion. Unverifiable means that the religion has correctly placed its beliefs in a realm where they cannot be contradicted.

A worse option is disproven.

4.7611 As religions codify and compete with other types of knowledge, like science, they learn to discard those of their assertions that can be disproven. Most of Christianity has quietly, in response to knowledge about the development of the Earth and Universe, abandoned the claims of a literal reading of Genesis. The Church holds on to those beliefs, however, that are unverifiable.

4.762 Unverifiable in religion is to science as the unstructured world is to projects. It is completely out of the line of fire. For the logical positivists, unverifiable was a badge of shame, because it also meant unprovable.[47] Yet this misses the fact that, for religion, unverifiable is a safe haven. Unverifiable is where a religion wants its beliefs to be when time has winnowed out the things that gradually are disproven.

4.763 Sometimes people try to "prove" religion rather than disprove it, or at least justify it through wisdom. To this extent they are making it something other than a belief system.

4.77 I can reject religion when it is shown that it lacks proof. But I need not. Belief is the finish line of a belief system. If I cross it, it doesn't matter how I got there.

4.78 Believing something doesn't make it true.

This is the case with all sorts of knowledge, not just religious belief. I can learn, or teach, that the Thirty Years War ended in 1600. It didn't, and I can be corrected. I don't jettison history for that reason. I merely correct this statement.

Similarly, I can learn from the priest, as part of my religion, that "those who steal go to hell." I can decide I think this unlikely, and simply reject it. Religion can also teach me that (say) women are inferior to men. Observation on my part can suggest to me that this is untrue. This does not mean the whole system need be jettisoned, any more than history need be rejected when I am corrected about something.

4.79 Awareness of beliefs as beliefs rather than as collectively shared knowledge typically increases someone's willingness to question them. Suddenly we are bothered by the fact that these things are unproven.

4.791 I call this sudden crossing of an invisible boundary where abruptly we no longer take for granted the water holding up our boat "looking at something with amazement." Abruptly it seems odd to us.

Amazement is behind all questions. How odd it is that "bring me a muffin" produces a muffin! How, we might wonder, do words mean?

How odd that God, whom we are taught to think of as unchanging, created the Earth and everything upon it. Does this mean He changed? Got lonely?

How odd that the self doesn't fly apart into pieces! What unifies it?

4.792 No one can say when amazement will occur, if it ever does. Our default position is to accept the world, not to find it odd. Nonetheless we are constantly finding specific things odd.

For every thing we find odd, we are accepting an infinity of other things.

4.7921 The fact that something seems odd to us doesn't mean it must seem so to someone else.

4.7922 It is possible to regard anything with amazement.

4.7923 Amazement seems to other people to come from nowhere. Abruptly we are not satisfied, when others are. This is so because amazement is always a fact of the personal world. Its social expression is the attempt at changing the world. From the point of view of the individual, amazement may be perfectly justifiable, a long time coming.

4.793 Religion is something personal, publicly disseminated. Science is something public, publicly disseminated. Situational knowledge is something personal that isn't disseminated at all.

Learning

4.8 What I know is a patchwork of things I have learned and things I have discovered.

4.81 I know that the earth is round. I know that Leonardo da Vinci painted "La Giaconda (Mona Lisa)." I know that the Thirty Years War ended in 1648. I know that matter exists in a mirror relationship to anti-matter.

4.811 Information such as this is taught to me. It is rare to be aware of the fact that initially people were not taught this information, but had to discover it.

4.812 We tend to be conscious of things we ourselves have discovered for longer than we are of things we have been taught. For others they merely form part of the world. They are facts. This is the reason why our "education" fades so quickly into the background.

Most of us discover only personal things, things of no interest to others. Very few of us ever discover anything that others want, like penicillin or a better mousetrap.

4.82 Each of us is the tip of an iceberg of all those who have gone before us, as we will become part of the iceberg of our successors. For ourselves, we are the end of it all; to others, we become like the mulch in which they, the new flowers, grow.

4.821 The quest for a reputation that lives on past our death is the attempt to separate out the things in this mulch that we have been the first to discover for special consideration, perception of them as things done, things discovered.

Such immortality is based on things of interest to others. There is no intrinsic difference between things of interest only to ourselves and things of interest to others. This means that most people cannot hope to be, in this sense, immortal.

This we may call the pagan sense of immortality. No wonder Christianity gained popularity as it found another way to be immortal, a much more (so to say) democratic one.

4.822 The quest for immortality through others is doomed to failure.

Though others can acknowledge our immortality momentarily, say by learning our name as the author of X, the discoverer of Y, they can never do it in the way we really want them to: by acknowledging us as the tip of such an iceberg as we seem to ourselves.

4.823 To others, these things are merely facts. Even if they learn them it is as things learned, not as things discovered. They don't really matter.

4.8231 Reading newspaper obituaries is a salutary exercise. This person's reason for inclusion was that she was "secretary to Congressman X," this person's that he was involved with a television show in the 1950s.

Even the outsider can see how painfully little of the person's life is covered: the person *is* the tiny moment of intersection with the public world.

4.824 Most of the things we do presuppose the things we have learned, but no longer are aware that we have learned. Intermixed with these are things we are in the process of learning. While we are learning them they are front and center; after we have learned them they fade, taking their place among the shadowy things we can no longer even distinguish. They become something we take for granted, like knowing how to cut open a package of chicken. We know where to find the knife, how to turn the oven on, where to throw the plastic, know to wash our hands afterwards. We merely do these things.

At any given time, our knowledge is arranged in a scale of importance to ourselves, usually related to how recent their acquisition was.

Expectations

4.9 Beliefs overlap with expectations.

4.91 We tend only to articulate beliefs and expectations when we run into problems carrying out our projects. Articulation of belief is almost always followed by a "but"—a reason for calling that belief into question.

So too for expectation: if our expectations are fulfilled we almost never articulate them. We articulate expectations with which we have had, or expect, some difficulties.

4.911 Expectations are the water under our boat. So long as the hull clears, it doesn't matter how deep the water is. This is not an issue, only the interface of the water with the boat.

Only the danger of not having enough water makes us question its depth.

4.92 It's by definition impossible to list all of our beliefs and expectations. Before the fact we have no reason to, and after the fact we become aware of the logical impossibility of doing so.

Expectations are related to beliefs.

I get up from bed in the middle of the night to go to the bathroom. Here, we might say I expect (believe) many things. I expect that my feet will meet solid flooring. I expect that they will be cushioned by a rug. I expect the sill will be there. I expect the bathroom will be there. I expect the sink will be there. I expect the sink is made of a hard substance. I expect the toilet will flush when I push the handle. I expect that mermaids will not come gushing out of the tap when I turn on the water.

But we'd never say any of these, any more than we can or would list all our beliefs. We'd probably never say, I expect the bathroom to be there when I go through the door—unless one day it hadn't been.

We never know how deep the water under our boat is.

4.921 We only articulate beliefs when we have a reason to. They are defined negatively.

4.93 Belief isn't a state, except when it's moved front and center, as in religion. Things are moved front and center one by one. This means that when one is, all the others remain in obscurity, or are pushed aside.

4.931 The same is true for doubt, that Descartes made central to his thought.[48] We can stop everything and doubt; sometimes we have to. But we can equally well not make doubt our central project. Plenty of people haven't, after all. Their boats float too.

4.932 What is moved front and center can by definition be moved back where it came from, or not moved to begin with.

4.9321 We don't have to answer the questions posed by philosophers in order to carry on with life. Life carries on perfectly well by itself. (See 0.1.)

4.94 Just as we can't say beforehand what all our beliefs are, so we can't sufficiently load our description of what must happen in the future with caveats to be sure of it happening in the way we want it to happen.

4.941 Macbeth was delighted to be told by the witches that he couldn't be defeated by someone "of woman born," nor before Burnham Wood should come to Dunsinane.[49] He thought both were impossible, and we can see his point. They are, if we add enough caveats to their understanding. For Macbeth, the emphasis was on "woman," not on a technicality regarding "born." For Macbeth (and probably for us), a "wood" was defined as roots in the ground. In fact it was cut-off branches that came to Dunsinane. This is not what we usually mean by a "wood."

4.9411 We can understand Macbeth's outrage, his sense that the witches had pulled a trick on him. We can imagine him howling, "But it isn't fair!" Even today, it does seem impossible for a person to come to be without the intermediary of a woman (test tube babies might be the counter-example, though the egg at one point, or what was used to clone it, will have come from a woman). Equally impossible, if we define trees as stuck fast, is forests changing place.

But who says that when things fail to work out, it is for a reason we foresaw? By definition, this will never be the case. If we could foresee the contingency, we could rule it out in our definition (as here, the witches ought have said: Careful! this prophecy does not include people born through Caesarian section).

4.9412 All surprises are precisely that: surprises. All descriptions of the future are attempts to protect ourselves against surprises.

By definition we can never protect ourselves against surprises. If we could, they wouldn't be surprises.

The Gordian knot could not be untied, but it could be cut, which wasn't at all what people had in mind. Still, for Alexander, who cut it, the problem was solved, and he moved on to other things. We can imagine those who tied the knot protesting violently: That isn't what we meant! It isn't fair!

4.942 When I say, the bathroom will be there when I get up at night, I'm not mentally ruling out specific exceptions, any more than Macbeth was conscious of ruling out exceptions like Caesareans or cut branches. They just didn't occur to him. Perhaps there's no way he could have known about them—say a scientist from a time machine was offering cloning down in England. Certainly I don't know everything that is possible, somewhere on Earth, nowadays, in Berkeley or one of the Cambridges.

4.943 Only when something isn't there am I aware of my belief and expectation that it would be. These beliefs and expectations are what differentiates this something that isn't there from the billions of other things that aren't there either, but whose absence I do not remark.

We remark the dog not barking, as in Sherlock Holmes, only if the dog should have barked.[50]

4.95 What if the bathroom were not there when I got up? I would have to explain this.

When expectations are contravened, I have to go about searching for the reason why. Explanations might include an earthquake (if I am a sound sleeper) or a vast and complex practical joke, or the bank taking back something that belonged to it in the middle of the night. If I had said, I know the bathroom will be there, and it isn't, say because of an earthquake, I would probably say: Oh well, except of course for earthquakes. Let's say the bathroom "wasn't there" for some other reason: I couldn't see it, say. Like Macbeth, we might wail, But it isn't fair! That isn't what I meant at all!

4.951 In the moment when we are confronted with something contrary to our belief and expectations, we are at point zero with respect to explanations.

In arriving at an explanation, we have available to us the whole spectrum of what we call subjective and objective explanations. We choose from all of them. None is outlawed before the fact. It may be I'm in a high fever and just think the bathroom isn't there. It may be it really isn't. If I decide the reason is an earthquake, there has to be a hole in the ground, or I revise my thesis.

4.952 The endless worrying of a Locke over whether what we think we see is us or "it," the outside world, was merely Locke's preoccupation.[51] This means, it need not be ours. The topic only comes up if there is a reason for it to come up, and when it does, the whole scale from subject to objective is available to us as explanations—we have to learn when to use which ones. We can't say beforehand which explanation will seem more appropriate. We use all the resources of our language. These resources are at our disposal because others have put them there. We can't use resources that aren't there, though we can steer a course between ones that are there to articulate a new one.

4.9521 If we read Locke in a philosophy class, we may well say, "How interesting!" But the problem doesn't really affect us.

This reaction re-weaves the shroud of philosophy. Academic philosophy consists of studying mummies.

4.96 Every person asking a question seriously thinks it needs to be answered. Those asking a question adamantly think that life cannot go on until that question is answered. (See 0.33.)

This is divertingly like the belief of the Aztecs that, when their two calendar cycles converged, as they did every 60-some years, the fires of the earth had to be re-started to prevent the end of the world. To ensure the world would not end, the heart had to be ripped from a sacrificial victim and a fire started with friction in the empty chest cavity. Then house fires, which had been doused, could be re-lighted, and the Earth would once again be saved.[52]

The Aztecs did this each time, and were always proved right in their belief: the world was saved, every time.

4.961 It is only because we are not asked to participate in Aztec beliefs that this can be used as an ironic example.

4.97 Much of Anglo-American philosophy of the last century has been devoted to worrying about how words function. It is as if we had to answer this before we could go forward.

This is comparable to the way that Modernist aesthetics insisted that without artists, we couldn't even perceive the world. (See 3.531.) You need us, they insisted! Philosophy has to decide "how words mean" before they can mean!

As if the whole edifice hangs in the balance between crumbling or not crumbling until it's decided how words mean.

Yet what allowed us to have this conversation if we had to figure out how words meant before they could mean? Or whether they meant at all? (Perhaps they don't; what would that change?)

By the twenty-first century, these questions about the nature of language have largely been abandoned, like questions about the extension of angels. It turned out we didn't have to have an answer to go forward after all. To listen to those debating at the time, however, we'd never have known this. They may have told us we were stupid if we weren't as worried as they. And now they're dead and gone, and somehow the questions have gone away. Poof!

4.971 We never know that actually it's not true the Big Questions have to be answered if all we hear is the insistence by a group of people that they alone have identified the Most Basic Question of all. To them, it may seem so. But with time and a new generation, it is unlikely it will seem so.

4.972 What "everybody" says matters for this reason is always wrong. Wait a generation, or even perhaps a few decades, and this becomes clear. The problem is waiting out their time of blundering and bellowing.

4.9721 The lure of language philosophy came from having an experience of amazement with the fact that saying to someone "bring me a muffin" produced a muffin. (See 4.791.) Or at least it sometimes did. If it didn't, we had to decide:

Was the person deaf, not Anglophone, busy, disrespectful, or unaware of the meaning of the word "muffin"?

This set of questions is like any set of Most Basic questions. It seems the More Basic questions are, the more they beg to be solved. It seems more is riding on figuring them out.

Actually, the More Basic they are, the less they beg to be solved because they're so basic. What do we imagine is going to happen whatever we decide about them? Will the world vanish in a puff of smoke?

4.9722 Maybe words don't mean. After all, "bring me a muffin" can fail to produce a muffin. Perhaps the person just doesn't feel like bringing one, or doesn't like our tone of voice.

Philosophy waves these things away: "Of course this doesn't apply to people who don't speak English or don't know what a muffin is! Don't you even know how philosophy works? I of course mean: assuming the person speaks English, knows what a muffin is, isn't deaf... and so on. I assume that you do get your muffin and hence that words do in fact mean. How do they mean? I mean, meaning in the abstract."

The point is precisely that we can't assume. If we don't get the muffin, we have to set to work to explain why not. So in almost all cases we may in fact get no "meaning" at all, and have to troll for an explanation (that we may never get). Quite a bit of the world apparently carries on without meaning at all.

4.97221 A comparable situation is the way we worry about what unifies the self. We assume it's unified. What unifies it?

In fact it may not be unified. Certainly there's as much evidence to suggest I'm disunified as unified.

Whatever I am, I am.

This is the sense, as Wittgenstein realized, that philosophy creates its own problems. It makes a statement and then worried about how this can be so. In fact it may not be so; whatever is is so, and it's not going to change based on what we say is so.

4.9723 It may have seemed that language, being the medium of thought, was the Most Basic issue. This was so only because people regarded the fact of language with amazement. Suddenly it seemed strange.

Anything can seem abruptly strange.

4.9724 For some earlier ages, the fate of the soul at death was the Most Basic issue. Or the nature of Christ: Human? Divine? Both? If both, how? We didn't solve these problems; we simply declared them resolved, which is something different—like a court producing a finding. The case is closed.

This rarely convinces the losing side.

4.9725 Have we ever explained the nature of the person? And yet people carried on.

Some people believe that only now have we attained an explanation of how the brain works. Earlier people lacked this knowledge.

Perhaps this is so, but somehow they carried on anyhow.

4.9726 The fact that we're amazed doesn't mean what amazes us has to be explained for things to carry on: anything can be regarded with amazement, and we can't explain everything, because we'll never access everything. Besides, there are many things to do with an hour besides explain.

Explanation is a specific action.

4.973 Literary theory in the U.S. was dominated for decades in the late twentieth century by Derrida, then by Foucault. Woe betided the person who wanted to, talk about something else other than the same thing, over and over: Derrida says this, Foucault says that. How essential they were made to seem, like referring everything to Marx and Lenin in East Germany before the fall of the Wall.

Yet the more absolutely a world is characterized by X, the more certain it is it will one day turn to Y. How funny the '50s look to us now! Or the '60s! They look funny now because they were as they were. They were something definite.

The more definitely "something" something is, the more certain that we will be able to turn to something else.

4.98 We can't ever solve all problems. We can't even solve specific ones; we merely abandon them.

Is scientific knowledge objective?

5 Science is knowledge as independent of any particular situation as possible.

5.1 Science is two separate things. It is the prow of the boat, always pushing forward into uncharted waters, and it is the record of the wake. Research in a laboratory is quite different to a scientist from teaching known facts to students.

5.11 Confusion is created by the fact that frequently the same person does both, research and transmission of the results of research. Even when people take one job or the other, both seem like science compared to, say, being a plumber.

5.12 To some degree, the wake dissipates over time, becoming part of the water. What was once the domain of science enters the daily world, becomes mere facts. For example the circumference of the Earth, or the speed of light, or what causes lung cancer. In other cases we can't use the findings of science in our daily lives and don't learn it. The information it uncovers remains in the domain of specialists.

5.121 There is no intrinsic difference of type between these two sorts of knowledge.

5.2 Science exists as a kind of knowledge only by contrast to knowledge that is not science. This is why it is wrong to think that everything can or should become science.

5.3 Science is not the gold standard of knowledge, it is a specific thing done. (See 4.22.) It is developed, and used, on an as-needed basis.

Science is knowledge that becomes so abstract with respect to the everyday mutable world that it suddenly congeals into something else. All scientific concepts represent a departure from everyday ones. "Everyday" will vary according to the world in which they are developed.

Everyday cannot, by definition, be scientific.

5.31 Science achieves generality by expressing it in terms of new, or hidden, or known-only-to-the-initiated particulars. Frequently we have to invent the vocabulary of science. The words mean what scientists say they mean.

This is what makes science a technical discipline; its terms remain to be defined. They don't trail associations of use like other words.

Mathematics is even more uncontaminated than science.

5.311 The world of science floats under, over, and in between the reality we take for granted, a world of "atoms" and "forces" and "waves" that, by dint of being another world in another vocabulary, can explain the everyday world we perceive.

These are general only by contrast with the way we expressed the world before. Compared to subsequent explanations, they may be particulars. This necessitates more science.

5.312 There is no intrinsic force pushing situational knowledge to become scientific. Making this change requires making an investment of energy, one which usually we have no reason for making.

5.313 In order to turn situational knowledge, at one end of the spectrum, into scientific knowledge, at the other end, we have to boil down the personal world. The result is something with only the most tenuous of connections to what went into its making. Nor can we always accomplish this boiling down: the way to do it must be discovered, or have been discovered.

5.314 We can construct a scientific statement out of the fact that at this particular point in time I was able to enter the traffic flow, and either did or didn't. Because we have some general knowledge of the vocabulary currently used for scientific statements, we would probably talk about speed and vector force, acceleration and friction. But what would the statement be?

Perhaps we would say, an object weighing just what my car weighs, under conditions just like those which obtained in this particular situation, with other bodies going at just these speeds (and so on), with this degree of traction on the road (do we have a measure of traction? If not we can come up with one, perhaps by breaking down "traction" into other things) will be able to enter this hole without encountering another body in motion.

This is a trumped-up exercise. We can use vocabulary developed out of other circumstances for this one. But why? This isn't the situation that produced these principles, and there's nothing in it that requires their use. Things like the smells and the colors of the cars, not to mention the feel of the experience, would be lost in this process of boiling down.

5.315 Science is an explanation system useful in fixing problems. Most of the time it's simply not required because we lack the problem that creates the necessity for science. We invoke science when the fabric of life snags, not when it unrolls seamlessly. Science offers explanations. If we don't need explanations, we don't do science.

5.316 Here's another example of the gulf between experience and science. Let's ask, What are the scientific principles behind *Rigoletto*?

Huh? we say. It isn't even clear what's being asked. Do we mean, the physics of how the stage holds up? The acoustics of how the sound travels? We aren't asking for an explanation of anything, so the principles merely float. They may be true, but we don't need them. Besides, we can only speak knowingly of physics and acoustics because these have been developed independently of *this* experience. We can't go directly from this experience sitting in the theater to "science." And how far from the actual experience is the abstraction! Of course this is so. This is the nature of the way things are.

5.312 We only have the scientific terms we have. If we hadn't developed terms for acceleration and so on, we wouldn't use these to give a scientific version of this situation. Terms we don't yet have we can't yet use.

5.318 Science has to be made. Making terms changes our conception of the world. They change the way we express it.

Scientific explanations

5.319 Science explains what is in common currency by appealing to, or constructing, layers. It takes virgin vocabularies and places them in the unseen places of our ordinary world: the microparticles we don't see, the macropatterns we cannot perceive. It invents special machines to see things that were there all along, but invisible to us. Leewenhoek's microscope, that found "beasties" in a drop of water, is emblematic of all science.

5.3191 We don't know and can't say how many such hidden worlds there are, because by definition they remain hidden until they are discovered.

5.32 Science produces explanations. Explanations go one layer beneath the layer we already have access to. If they don't, they're not explanations. Not all explanations are scientific.

5.321 "Dad, why can't I go to the prom?" "Because you can't" is not an explanation. "Because you're only 16 and kids going to the prom are 18" *is* an explanation. It delineates two categories: those who go to the prom and those who don't, based on age. It gives the underlying structure of things.

"Why do we become forgetful when we age?" "Because that's part of ageing" is not an explanation. "Because X, Y, and Z" happens in our brains *is* an explanation.

"Because I said so" is also an explanation. It says, what the parent says is different from what other people say. It is always followed.

5.33 Explanations typically replace the layer they are underneath. When we have explained ageing through synapses and electric jolts in the brain, we may say this *is* ageing.

In some cases, however, science exists parallel to everyday use. We still speak of the sun "rising" and "setting" even though the scientific explanation involves the abstractions of planets and heavenly bodies. Perhaps people will still "age" even when we can explain the phenomenon, but we will think of these old-fashioned terms as figures of speech. If our scientific terms are ever themselves explained, they in turn will become the figures of speech.

5.4 The scientific vocabulary of reproducibility and generalizability (X will always do Y under circumstances Z) is what separates it from the mutable world. It deals with entities that transcend the mutable: platelets, say, or orbits, or waves, or light-years.

5.41 If platelets and orbits become the vocabulary of the masses used to describe the everyday, to this extent they cease to be science, and become merely facts. The popularization of science is always its death knell, as well as the sign of its greatest success. (See 5.12.)

5.42 All conclusions are responses to specific questions, and are based on limited data.

5.421 It should be no surprise that some of what scientists told us once is now seen to be false, such as that masturbation was harmful, or that non-white races were inferior to white.

5.4211 Now it seems outrageous that data which would have disproven these assertions was excluded or overlooked. Such data would have included considering people who masturbated and were not weak-minded, or intelligent members of non-white races. But being outraged at exclusion means we have not understood that most of the world at any given time is excluded and overlooked. This is not a correctable fault. It is only correctable if we are living at the end of time.

5.42111 We can demand that these data be considered, but we cannot legitimately demand that others have looked at all possible data.

5.42112 We can say it was illegitimate to exclude data, or we can give a name to the reason, say racism. But this does not mean that the science was "bogus."

In the same way that we live in error most of our lives, science is always in error. (See 1.1.) We correct our personal errors; science corrects its errors. Correcting errors is doing science; they can never be eliminated.

Science is a manner of proceeding. It is an activity. It the other sense it is merely what this activity, at a given time, produces.

5.42113 We change science by asking it to generalize based on new data, or unconsidered data. Of course its results will alter as well.

5.5 Having expectations contravened allows us to say what these expectations were to begin with.

5.51 We have to be struck by something unusual to look for an explanation. Pasteur was struck by the lack of mold in his Petri dish.

"Why are the seagulls sitting on the lampposts?" is probably not a question leading to scientific inquiry. We think we know the answer: they're resting, and the lampposts are available. "Why are all the seagulls facing the same way?" may lead to scientific answers. Perhaps we will discover atmospheric conditions, or wind patterns that no one knew to exist. Or maybe that seagulls know when something is interesting to look at it. If this led to a new understanding of seagulls, this would be science. If it didn't, it wouldn't be.

5.52 Science never explains the ordinary, because the ordinary, being ordinary, doesn't seem to require an explanation. This is what leads to the strangeness of top-down attempts to superimpose science on specifics that don't demand them, such as asking what the science of entering traffic might be.

5.53 It's always a decision to look for an explanation. The default of life is *not* looking for an explanation. Every demand for an explanation upsets the apple cart. Things seemed fine before.

5.531 Those who think an explanation necessary only do so because they have in a sense already begun looking for it. Frequently they criticize those who are not looking for this explanation: why are they sitting on their hands?

We can't look for every explanation, any more than we can articulate all our beliefs, our justify them.

We can justify certain ones, or look for certain explanations, but during that time a thousand million things go by that do not have an explanation, and for which we look for none. (See 4.9726.)

5.54 To go from looking for specific explanations, which mankind has always been capable of, to codifying this activity as a public undertaking, took a leap of imagination. Generally speaking, it seems that Western man after the Greeks and before the Renaissance had not made this leap.

Once people figured out how to do this, it seemed self-evident, and they looked with pity on the people who didn't do it. But many people today resist this way of thinking. This too is a specific way of doing things.

5.541 The Church already had explanations. It wasn't looking for them. Of course the Church opposed science, but not because of the particular nature of its dogmas.

The beliefs of a religion or any belief system are fixed. The results of science are constantly changing, as science is an activity. The fixed opposes the changing.

5.55 Science discovers the objective world. But what makes the world, and science, objective, is the assumption that the world is there to be discovered.

5.56 This means, that explanations are there to be discovered. We may not discover them, and our children may not discover them, nor their children. Still we hold that they are there to be discovered. In this sense the belief is unverifiable because it cannot be disproven.

Outsiders sometimes speak of the "religion of science."

5.57 Sometimes we don't know where to look, so we just start looking. This is called pure research. We hope that somehow what we discover will come in useful some day.

5.6 A scientific question is a question at the edge of the known. That means, of the generally known.

5.61 At any given place in this sequence of things I did not know, the reason could have been something with or requiring a scientific explanation.

5.611 Science is the really big guns. Usually little guns are more than sufficient in the daily world. That's why we call it the daily world.

5.612 Just as we don't usually solve financial woes by winning the lottery, it's rare when we need to invoke science to solve our problems, especially not in the "prow of the ship" sense: new science. This is so because of the very nature of how it is constructed. Most of the explanations we require in the world are in the form of the things we as a collective already know.

5.62 The situation of not knowing that leads to science doesn't look any different to the individual than the situation that does. Who could have said beforehand that the mold in Pasteur's Petri dish would have been of scientific interest?

5.621 If we have a problem, first we just we ask around. Some problems are things that only I fail to know the answer to but everybody else does know. Such as, what is this scratching sound on my roof at night? My situation of not knowing was not the situation that produces science. Or rather, I didn't know if it was, but assumed it wasn't. It had a "normal" explanation, an everyday one, one that our vocabulary could take care of.

The scratching noise on my roof could have been the noise of a strange disintegration of the tiles caused by Martian rays. Science would have been very interested in this indeed. But of course this is not likely.

5.6211 People tend to hope that they will be the one case in a million. Usually they aren't.

5.622 I may lack an explanation for something that one of my friends knows. Someone in the big city may know the answer to a question that no one in my town knows. But if we find a question that, asking around, we discover to be unanswerable by anyone, we have found a question that science can go to work on.

5.63 Science may involve solitary work, but what makes this solitary work scientific is its place in the larger whole.

5.631 There is no intrinsic difference between figuring out a problem of only personal interest and figuring out a problem of general interest, such as science devotes itself to. You have to ask the general to see if the problem is of general interest.

5.6311 This is an aspect of science that Charles Peirce was aware of. Its nature is defined by its place in the social whole. Peirce over-reached his point, however, by saying that science was something that could only be done collectively. In fact, it is quite possible for an individual working alone to make a discovery that the collective sees as a major scientific discovery. It's trivial to say that we aren't a great writer, or scientist, until others say we are, if this is only so by definition. We can still do what we do in solitude. Of course the chances are wildly against the subsequent canonization of a product produced in absolute solitude. But it isn't theoretically impossible. The nature of science is determined by the nature of the world. It's determined by what we know.

5.632 When the third grade feeds one set of plants water and the other a noxious household chemical, this is not science. "We" know what the outcome will be, even if the third grade doesn't. If it isn't produced, then something has gone wrong. To the third graders, it looks like science.

Science is socially defined in the sense that the questions of science don't look any different than a million other questions we ask. What makes scientific questions different is that for the questions of science, we don' have explanations. We collectively, that is. Not, those in the third grade. No one, at least not in the group that for us defines our world.

Martians might, but we don't have access to them.

5.633 What makes science science is, first, that no one knows the answer to the question. Second, the question must be one many people want to know the answer to.

The question, "Why is my father so difficult to get along with?" is not a question for science because no one but me is interested in my father, not because of the form of the question. Unless he is in some way one of a kind.

If my father is the King, it's conceivable that he could be considered one of a kind. In the eyes of modern medicine, kings and queens are medically the same as other people. In the Middle Ages he would have been thought different. And nowadays, for the gossip sheets, he would be thought different. If my father is a Martian, we're interested in him scientifically even now.

5.634 In the same way, we're interested in questions about what we call "the" sun, "the" moon. They are still particular enough that data about them count as science. If there were a thousand moons around Earth, and we had samples of rocks from all of them, we would not say that analyzing rock samples from any of them, unless it was in some way out of the ordinary, counted as science.

5.635 Having a blood test isn't science, though it may use techniques developed by science.

5.64 The process of coming up with an explanation that answers our questions occurs in fits and starts. Sometimes we have the questions for a long time before we have the answers. Sometimes we have the answers, that is to say the raw data, long before we realize that they offer answers to questions we have. Sometimes we are actively looking for answers to questions and keep discarding contenders.

5.65 Explanations cause the world to recede by the thickness of only one layer. We can't skip levels of explanation and go four levels of explanation below where we are right now. This is so by definition. Explanation is always an explanation to a particular problem or set of problems in the layer we have.

5.651 Because science is that enterprise at the edge of the world that people have answers to, one of its edges faces the void. It's always possible some day to ask for an explanation for this layer of explanation.

For now, we may be satisfied with saying that, say, memory is the firing of brain synapses. One day someone may ask, "Why do the brain synapses fire this way to produce memory?" And we will have to begin work on yet another layer of explanation.

5.652 In order to find this most general layer, science will have to invent yet newer vocabularies, delve into yet further realms that have not already been colonized. For if they had been colonized, someone would have come up with this as the explanation that was wanted, and they wouldn't have had to be discovered.

5.66 Science is what's left standing when everyone has had a shot at it. This means, by definition what is still standing is something no one who's tried can show to be wrong. If it can be shown to be wrong, it isn't science. That's the process of what we call verification.

5.661 Yet verification, or verifiability, is not what sets science apart from other undertakings.

There is no such thing as the "scientific method." Kant was right, in a sense: this is the way we look for explanations and find solutions to problems. It's the way our mind works.[53] (Not looking for solutions to problems is always an option.) We use this method for daily life, not just science.

5.662 At the same time it's easy to understand why scientists would call this the "scientific method," and act as if science invented it. Science by definition is self-conscious methodologically. It has to be, because it is a game that in theory is open to anyone who is able to play it. If you don't define the players, you have to define the nature of the game.

5.663 In this way science is very democratic: anybody who can play the game can play it.

5.664 Because it is a sort of activity rather than a content, in its early centuries almost anyone could engage in it. Because the questions that "we" fail to know the answers to have become more specialized in these fields, these particular branches of science are nowadays only for specialists.

5.6641 This is probably what Peirce meant when he suggested that science actually made the world more regular.[54] We know more answers.

5.6642 Yet Peirce was wrong to think that this meant that science somehow regularized and in a sense used up the world.

Peirce was comparing the regular bales spit out by the threshing machine to the unthreshed field: some day it would all be threshed. But we can't oversee the whole field. Science is only regular compared to what's going into the thresher, not with respect to the field.

5.66421 By definition science is only with respect to what is: it comes to be by contrast with the everyday world. If we have the everyday world, as we always will, given that science is only science by contrast with it, we have the possibility for science.

5.66422 People wishing to engage in scientific activity without investing in the hugely specialized paraphernalia that has developed must ask unanswerable questions of different sorts, about different kinds of things. They must create new realms.

5.6643 Science solves particular problems we encounter in the everyday world.

The value of science is not intrinsic, it is with respect to the everyday world that causes it to be evoked.

5.665 We don't have to justify science any more than we have to justify talking, or singing.

5.666 Scientists aren't other kinds of creatures. They like (say) flowers and chardonnay and have to put out the garbage. That doesn't stop for the laboratory.

5.6661 Scientific reasoning occurs as part of a dense thicket of reasoning identical to it save only that what I'm doing isn't science (others aren't interested in it, and/or it concerns things we know already). But the reasoning is unchanged, whether it is scientific or one of its several first cousins. (See 5.661.)

5.6662 When I put my house on the market, I had to replace the ceiling tiles in the downstairs "mother-in-law" apartment kitchen, which were spotted. There were many things about this undertaking that I had learned from doing it the first time. For example that ceiling tiles simply pushed up and out (this was not a scientific discovery, because there are many people who know this), that they can be cut neatly if you run the knife down the back but are very messy to cut if you do it on the face meant to be seen (technicians know this, and most people who have tried themselves). I had even discovered which hardware supply store to go to get new ceiling tiles, and was savvy enough from my first visit there to insist that they did too sell them singly, despite what the salesman told me the second time. This is probably situational knowledge.

My problem then became, how to get the grid over the ventilation pipes back up? It hung upside down, attached to the vent by two screws. The hole the screw went into had been made manually with a nail, and the metal of which the vent chute was made was so flimsy that when I pushed up on the screw with the screwdriver, the flange bent back and the screw jittered out of the hole. I tried reaching from the side, around the already-installed ceiling tiles. My arm wasn't long enough. How to accomplish this? What was causing the flange to buckle each time? I had to come up with a thesis, and decide whether it was correct. Was it the angle of the screw? The pressure I was putting on it? What was the determinative factor here? Many sweaty minutes later, I gave up in a huff. When I had cooled down I had an idea: perhaps a longer screw would solve the problem. I drove to the hardware store, not even knowing if such a screw existed, found one, and in seconds had put it in on my arrival home.

This thought was not scientific, because the problem was only my own, and it was what we call a practical one. But all the thought patterns were the same as those of a scientist in a laboratory. I meet resistance, I come up with a hypothesis regarding the source of the resistance, I try to eliminate irrelevant variables, I test my hypothesis. What I took to be the reason for my success (screw too short) need not have been so, but only piggybacked on the real reason (threads stripped on the old one)—something I could only find by further investigation, should I have been so inclined.

Since my goal was achieved, I had no reason to express general principles—how would I in any case have done so? There is nothing logically absurd about saying, what I discovered was how to put in this screw on this vent on this day in this house. Others aren't going to be interested. The knowledge was used up in the moment.

Yet the means of going about solving this problem was "scientific."

5.667 Any of these things not known could have defined a sub-group of questions. For that group, the attempt to answer the questions could have been science. But it wouldn't have been science from the point of view of those looking on from the outside.

5.67 What we call science with no further qualifiers is universal and international. If no one can answer the question, then the question is one of science.

5.68 Science is what's left on the table when the questions people can answer have been answered. This doesn't mean that what's on the table right now is what's always going to be on the table.

Possible worlds

5.7 Thinkers have spent many centuries worrying the problem of whether we can make scientific statements that will be true forever, and in all circumstances. This is a subset of the ongoing human need to attain surety. We usually associate this problem with Hume and Kant, and see it continue to play out in thinkers like Karl Popper.[55] Do we know the sun will rise tomorrow? Is induction valid? And so on.

5.71 This argument usually fires up when someone offers a statement he or she takes to be invariable for all time, and in all circumstances.

5.711 Sometimes we express this, echoing Leibnitz as parodied by Voltaire, by saying that X is true "in all possible worlds."[56]

We visualize the real world and then mentally change A, B, and C. We then think hard to figure out what changes this initial change implies. Perhaps we reason that D, E, and F will be different as well. Or G, H, and I. Finally we run out of things we think are linked to A, B, and C. This we proclaim to be a "possible world." And why not? Possible worlds by definition aren't the real world. If they are they're no longer possible. They're the world that is.

But let's say that A, B, and C did change. What makes us think that D, E, and F, or perhaps also G, H, and I, are in fact the only changes that will be made in such a world? Or any finite list? Perhaps one day the world will change in this way, and we will be shown to have been wrong. What will we say then? "Oops"?

When we say "possible world" we mean a mental construction we cannot show to be inconsistent with itself based on the evidence we have. It is possible compared to clearly impossible, not compared to reality. Maybe it isn't possible after all.

5.712 Many of the things we know to be true are not offered as candidates for scientific verities. No one would ever say, in all possible worlds this screw can be made to go in this hole in this flange in the duct cover by doing X and Y. It seems too specific.

5.7121 A report in the science column of the newspaper as I write this tells of the recent discovery of how insects known as water gliders move so quickly across the surface of the water. This is beyond the visibility of the naked eye and daily life and so it is legitimately in the domain of science. We learn that scientists have determined that these insects "row" with their middle legs. It happens so fast we can't see it. The scientists used special cameras and dyed water to make their discovery.

No one would propose that water gliders had to "row" with their middle legs in all possible worlds, whatever this phrase means. It seems too peculiar to our own world, now that we know what the situation is. Why can't they move in another way in another possible world and still be water gliders? It doesn't matter to us how they move, so we say: Sure, let them move differently. This is a permissible variable, a fact of content, not structure.

All we really mean is, we can't see it matters. Perhaps it does.

5.72 The strongest claims for what has to be true in all possible worlds are always expressed in the things furthest from what we take to be the accidental specifics of our world. A typical claim is that water will always be H2O in all possible worlds.

Saying that water will always in all possible worlds be H2O seems different from saying that water gliders will row with their middle legs in all possible worlds. In fact it is different, in that it is abstracted from everyday vocabulary. The vocabulary seems to us less that of content, something in the world, and more of structure. The further science gets from the ordinary, the more likely we are to speak in terms of what is necessary for "possible worlds."

5.721 Such arguments use as examples things so technical that the layer of explanation they involve has not been made quotidian, part of the content of the world rather than its structure. If it entered the world as content we wouldn't say that all possible worlds had to contain it. But this distinction is a malleable one, not an absolute one.

No one uses the Periodic Table of Elements for anything but the Periodic Table. It's not (or not yet) content; its use is still only as an explanation as to why certain things happen. Nor do we have serious contenders as to why the elements are as they are, or combine to form the substances they do. It's possible to ask, "Why?" of this, but we don't at the moment because we have no reason to.

Not asking "Why?" doesn't prove we won't some day, just that we haven't asked it yet.

5.722 If someone showed us how H20 could in fact fail to be water, we would conclude that this was a possibility, and the statement that water would always be H20 in all possible worlds would have to be qualified or revised.

Yet the assertion of those who claim that water must in all possible worlds be H2O will be, no one *can* ever show us this. What we are arguing over is whether we can take the most unassailable assertions of science and, in ways we cannot currently imagine, assail them.

If we can't imagine assailing them, we can't imagine assailing them. What we are arguing about is whether we can know something we don't know. We have so constructed the problem as to be unsolvable, and then we are bemoaning the fact that we cannot solve it.

5.723 When we argue over whether in all possible worlds H20 will be water, the fact that we are arguing means the question can't be answered here in the present, where we are arguing about it. It means we finally have a candidate that is general enough and sufficiently removed from the daily vocabulary of our world that we can see no reason it would be different.

The fact that we are able to get a good argument going is precisely what shows us its pointlessness. This is my way of expressing Wittgenstein's sense that we make our own problems.

Nobody argues about the water gliders.

At this point, "have not disproven" works as a synonym for "cannot disprove." We have to have a reason for separating these, only here we don't. Hence the argument.

5.724 We can have sympathy for Popper, who insists that the mere fact that something hasn't been disproved doesn't mean it can't be.[57] This is usually understood as saying, at some point it is possible it can be disproven. But actually all we know is that we don't know.

So this doesn't end up being any different from saying, this may turn out to be something so fundamental it will never be explained away or relativized, or it may turn out to be subsumed by another explanation layer. Because we don't have that explanation layer, we don't know.

The future has the last laugh. We can assert, here in the present, that we are sure of X, Y, and Z, which will never change. But we aren't in the future, any more than Macbeth was. We're here in the present, making assertions about the future, which is not the same thing as being in the future.

Objectivity

5.8 Nowadays, the argument between defenders and attackers of science consists in the attackers saying that science is after all subjective. This means, it's something people do. Its claims change.

5.81 This is the position of a historian of ideas, who simply backs away from the development of ideas far enough to see alteration.

5.811 The distance s/he must back before s/he sees alteration itself changes. Sometimes alteration comes quickly, sometimes slowly, so it does no good to say, everything changes. Sometimes that's true in short order. Sometimes, for very long periods of time, it isn't. And it's merely a belief to say that everything will change. What if we wait and wait, and it doesn't? Are we only vindicated centuries down the road when, finally, it does? Or were we wrong? Does it have to change within a certain period of time for us to have been right?

5.82 To say that science isn't objective sounds to scientists as if people were claiming they made it all up, as if they could say just anything. But scientists can't just say anything they feel like.

5.83 Science, to those doing it, feels like looking for something not found, not making it up. I can't say the explanation of cancer is "too much reading" or "too much broccoli" without having a reason for saying one of these, and experiments, to back up my contention.

Those trained in science are taught they can't just make things up, because the nature of scientific enterprise is that everyone may train all logical tools on our assertions to prove them wrong. But this is as much a matter of wisdom as of "scientific method." The chances against something I just made up standing up to public scrutiny are about as slim as the first monkey with the first typewriter typing out Shakespeare's works.

5.84 Most scientific assertions are made carefully, based on feedback from other people, and step by step piecing together of theories subjected to verification procedures. How can people who constantly have the sense of watching their step be sympathetic to thinkers who seem to place what they do on the same level with a tall tale?

5.85 Of course science is objective.

It is so because it's unlike the things that are subjective. Objectivity is found in the fact that science always insists explanations are possible, and that its assertions are what are left standing when individuals have taken their shots. In this sense science transcends the subjective.

5.851 Some people will say, this is still a subjective explanation of objectivity. The objectivity of the world is that it *really* exists, outside of us. Not because it's related to us, but because it isn't.

But that is its relation to us.

5.852 First this view separates us from the world, and then asks us to be reunited with it by a magic trick: the objective world has no relation to us. Except that this is just what makes it ours again.

This is like the way we wish for magic to make the stalled cars ahead of us simply disappear. (See 2.52.) We can identify our project, and the reality, and the chasm between them. The magic is what crosses this chasm.

The fact that the magic is necessary shows that it won't happen, not really. That's what magic is, something that isn't going to happen. If it does, it isn't magic any longer. It's part of the world.

This is probably what Wittgenstein meant, in the *Tractatus*, by saying "Die Welt ist alles, was der Fall ist." [58] If it happens, it's part of this world, not another one. The truck in front of us may disappear, but it won't be in a way we're expecting: there will be an explanation (it gets bombed from the air).

5.8521 It's because we are part of the world that we can separate subjective from objective.

5.853 The objectivity of science is founded on what science does and how it does it, all as part of the same world as subjectivity.

5.8531 Some scientists will try and prove the objectivity of science, or of the world. This is futile.

Science is objective because we hold it to be objective. No, say die-hards. It's objective regardless of what we hold.

This is the inescapable circle that makes us throw up our hands.

5.85311 For many scientists, the objectivity of the world is found in the fact that things have a specific explanation, this one explanation and not another. A person's smoking, it turns out, is correlated to his getting lung cancer, but his twiddling pencils isn't.

But why should this show the objectivity of the world more than the fact that my coffee cup is red rather than blue? Or that people have two arms rather than three?

The objectivity of the world in this sense turns out to be the same as merely that things are as they are. But what would it be if they weren't? They would still be as they are, whatever that would be.

When the way things are seems the proof of the objectivity of the world is only when we didn't know, or were surprised. Most of the time we aren't surprised, we just take things for granted.

5.9 People jut into the world. And that means, the shape of the world is dependent on us; our shape is dependent on the world. The relation is reciprocal.

5.91 The degree to which we and the world are related diminishes the further we get away from the membrane of intersection with the world.

5.911 If we had three arms, clothes would be different. Keyboards would be different, and probably household appliances. There would be different sports. Houses would be different to a lesser degree (stairs might be unaffected).

5.912 To say that Pike's Peak would not be affected by our having two arms or three means that it is further away from the membrane of intersection of the person with the outside world than shirts.

But we determine how far away things are precisely by seeing whether they would be affected, not the reverse. So we can't start off by saying how much they'd be affected. We have to look and see.

Besides, Pike's Peak might be affected after all. Certainly it's further from the world determined by our bodies than typewriters. Still, if we had three arms, its ascent might not be so difficult, and so it would loom less high in our imaginations. It might not be worth naming any more, the way we don't name individual bumps in the road, or individual anthills.

5.913 But, some people would be quick to say, the constitution of the blood wouldn't be different, or the brain waves produced by schizophrenia, or the chemical makeup of egg yolks. Water would always be H_2O. These at least seem far away enough from the normal world associated with people that they would not be affected by the number of our arms.

In the thought experiment we are running, it's true we can't see evident connections, even after serious thought. This is what it means to call these things part of the world outside of us (this may or may not be the same as the objective world: a shirt is still part of the objective world). But if suddenly we did wake up with three arms (by definition, this would be in a way we can't conceive of it happening), we might be surprised by the effects of the change. Even things far away from us might be affected in ways we can't say. We don't know what the ripple effects would be of having three arms. Then we would say "Oops."

Miracles

5.9131 Miracles are possible. Miracles are things happening in ways we haven't predicted. Such a miracle might be waking up with three arms. Or Burnham Woods coming to Dunsinane. Or the dratted truck in front of us suddenly vaporizing.

These are profound enough, because they remind us that by definition we never include the uncharted world in the map of our paths and projects. But they wouldn't satisfy the people for whom it's become an issue in itself to insist that "miracles are possible." They're not what these people mean.

For this sort of miracle, it doesn't really matter whether we say they're possible or not. We never mean, this particular "miracle" is possible, because if we could say how it worked, the miracle wouldn't be one. In the same sense, an explained magic trick isn't a magic trick any more.

5.9132 Most people invested in "believing in miracles" as an end in itself further add the caveat that this miracle must be inexplicable by physical means. If we wake up with three arms, we "can't see how they did it." The arm can't have been attached surgically. If it turned out we were genetically pre-disposed, as the first reported case ever, to grow an arm on this day in our life, it wouldn't be a miracle in the sense they demand miracles be. So the sense of "I don't know how it happened" is essential for those who "believe it happened."

5.9133 To which those who believe that everything is explicable by physical means (even if they haven't found the explanation) will say, not having an explanation means not having an explanation *yet*. We may have unexplained, but inexplicable is impossible.

5.9134 By definition, there's no way to distinguish intrinsically between "don't have an explanation yet" and "can't have an explanation." The difference is only whether or not we're looking for an explanation.

5.92 Anything that's so is part of the world.

5.921 Whatever it is, is what it is.

5.922 We always imagine with respect to what is. We're constantly running simulacra of situations in our heads. What if I cross the street here? What if I tell the boss off? What are the likely results of my having forgotten X or Y? Doing A or B? These aren't "possible worlds," they're merely attempts to list all the likely effects of specific things we can think of.

5.9221 Any single one, or all, of these effects, can fail to be produced. But if they weren't the usual effects of these things, we wouldn't think of them. So the fact that we think of these effects as possible doesn't say anything intrinsically about the effects, only says we thought of them.

5.9222 We learn what are usual effects. This is a form of wisdom. Specific bits of wisdom can be questioned, but not all wisdom can be questioned. There isn't time in the day, and we're doing other things.

5.9223 We could stand before each action and spin out to infinity the list of possible consequences. If we did this, we'd never act. We learn to confine our consideration to the most obvious layer, the next most-obvious layer, and then perhaps some things we alone think of. Then we act. No one can fault us for being careless, even if we turn out to have made the wrong decision. That's what it means not to be careless: not to be right, but to have looked at (say) three layers of possible effects. Other effects can always be hiding in the fourth, or indeed in the first.

5.92231 We learn to think of the things others think of. If we are clever, we throw in one or two more. But compared to all the things that could be thought of, all this is by definition a drop compared to Victoria Falls.

5.92232 We must strike a balance between dithering and being too hasty.

5.93 Trying to assign blame in a court case is a form of running the film again with only one element changed. If X had cleared his sidewalk, Y would not have slipped and fallen. Of course if X had cleared his sidewalk, Y might in that alternative world have gotten the notion to go around by a different route, and never slipped at all, so that the two might never have been connected. Or, given a cleared sidewalk, he might have been hit by a falling tree limb.

5.931 All of us play this game of "what if I had done things differently?" What if I had not looked away from the wheel to pay attention to something on the seat? Would the accident have been avoided?

5.9311 Being wise to the ways of the world means, being able to list most of the things most closely related to the change. It's possible to overlook changes very close to the change, but distant ripple effects always remain in a blur. That's why two people argue in a court case. As in science, everyone gets a shot. The one left standing is the winner.

A decision one way or another doesn't mean the one who won was right, only that s/he presented the better case. We don't win over the world as a whole, only over our human adversary, also a part of the world. If the thing actually happened, we could say who was right. But in this case it wouldn't be a possible world, but the actual one.

5.932 When we think of what might have been or what might be, the comparison we make is always to what happened. We never create an independently existing "possible world," only a version of the real world with specific qualities changed.

5.94 Robert Nozick offers a view of science that at first glance may seem like mine.[59]

Science, he and I agree, is something done, as well as a body of findings. The enterprise itself can't be true or false, because it's an activity. Its findings, however, can be true or false. Nozick accepts, as I do, that the enterprise of science consists of discarding things that had previously been held to be true.

5.941 For Nozick, objectivity is not an absolute quality, but one that admits of degrees.

He holds that what I as an individual know is related to science because both are admixtures of the same elements of subjective and objective, only in different amounts.

What I say is this: What only I know is different from science, though to be sure this is (only) because it is only I who knows it.

5.942 Nozick wants everyone to agree that scientific facts are merely more objective than other things, not objective *tout court*.

In fact, science is objective *tout court*. It is an activity constructed so as to fill this space on a continuum. Of course any particular product of science can fail to do this.

Nozick is selling short the truly different nature of scientific undertaking. Science requires people to give up the vocabulary we have learned to describe things in, and adopt new ones. The vocabulary of science is not personally constructed, but collectively. But it is a collective that goes at cross-purposes to the world we perceive.

5.943 The relation between kinds of knowledge is external, not internal as Nozick suggests. That is why it has to be pointed out. And nothing need necessarily be the result of becoming aware of this external linkage.

Nozick is trying to forge a compromise position that everyone will be willing to agree on. They will not do so. Why should scientists accept this Unitarian "everybody welcome" view of their undertaking if they can get Catholic certainty?

5.9431 Nobody need agree with anything I've said. Agreement is a separable issue, not the goal.

5.944 Objectivity and subjectivity, as well as the many states that mediate between them, sit in equal chairs along a line with no center and no head. But they are in different chairs.

Differences between things at different places of the scale are a result of their placement, as the difference between colors (according to current science) is the result of the speed at which their waves vibrate (an example of how science "explains" the world by creating entities whose place in the world has yet to be defined), even though this produces different effects in the visual world.

5.9441 We can *transform* what I know into science, given enough work. This transformation process means what I know will alter its form so that it is no longer what I know, but instead something we know. (See 5.3122.) But it is a transformation.

In the same way, my personal knowledge can become of general interest. Most of its particularity is burned away. I may well not recognize the result as mine. Or I may, but nobody else will.

In this way a novelist can say what the personal elements in a work of his or her fiction are. A reader won't know.

5.95 No absolute distinction of dual entities such as mind/body, subjective/objective, can end up being correct. By definition the two halves of the duality are related, or they wouldn't be linked pairs. And separating them will certainly produce the backlash of pointing out their similarity for that reason, as over-emphasis of one will almost certainly produce the backlash of pointing out the importance of the other.

5.96 Yet there may well be a reason we are drawn to the postulate of duality. It corresponds to the sensation we have of complete disconnect in the moment where, in Peirce's terms, "Firstness" contrasts with "Secondness." We sense "Secondness" when we bang our noses against a lamppost, say, or reach for something that isn't there. The world, it seems, has betrayed us.

5.961 We conceive of the world as external to ourselves when our expectations turn out to have been wrong. We bang into a lamppost where we thought there was nothing on the corner. But had there been nothing, as expected, we would have never thought of the lamppost that wasn't there.

5.97 We sometimes have the sense of oneness with the world too, complete boundarylessness, a kind of transcendental float. This is "Firstness." Our worldview may well be determined by the amount of pain inflicted on us: the stick ultimately seems more powerful than the carrot.

5.98 Peirce thought these two somehow naturally produced "Thirdness." Few people understand what this might mean.

I think in fact all we do is alternate between "Firstness" and "Secondness." Life is the alternation; there's nothing beyond these except their combination.

5.981 Combination isn't the same as duality. To sense combination we're looking down at both elements of the dualism. To sense duality we're on the same level as these.

What is the nature of social systems? Of democracy?

6 Collective projects comprise a social system.

6.01 The collective aspect of the project is the aspect that doesn't have to be constantly re-negotiated by individuals. As individuals, we don't have to pay attention to it. It is produced as the result of all our individual projects if everyone acquiesces in doing and not doing some of the same things.

We only pay attention to the problematic aspects of our project, not the aspects that aren't problematic.

This is not an objective distinction, but a subjective one. We can regard at any time any aspect as problematic. We regard it with amazement. (See 4.791.)

6.02 The ultimate project of a social system is the construction of the collective. Any collective, to be a project, dictates some actions by individuals.

6.03 It isn't correct to say that we agree to these limitations. Agreement is an actual act, a conscious state. Instead, we acquiesce. This is negative: we fail to regard these things with amazement. We fail to question them.

We accept them.

The problem with Rousseauean social contract theory was precisely that there wasn't ever a contract, a conscious agreement. So John Rawls re-introduced the social contract as a thought experiment: what we would have done if we were following his rules. [60]

But Rawls still doesn't go far enough in acknowledging the fictional nature of the social contract. It isn't there at all: thinking we need a contract to continue together is like saying we need a list of our beliefs and expectations. This is quite wrong. All we need is for people to not question certain things.

We don't need a social contract, real or imaginary, if we get the acquiescence that was to have been its effect.

6.031 Not questioning something is not the same as agreeing to it.

6.04 If we fail to acquiesce to these common limitations, differences within those parameters will take on the quality of absolute differences.

6.041 If we emphasize our differences to too great a degree, we may see no reason to act within the common parameters. We resist the limitations on actions that shared parameters necessarily imply.

If we do this, we will have lost sight of the collective project. This is always a possibility, though it may be one we wish to avoid.

You don't stop people from losing sight of it by telling them, in no matter how sophisticated a fashion, "But you agreed to this!"

6.042 The ultimate project of a traffic light is regulating traffic. How we stop, how we feel about stopping, what we do while we are stopped: all these things are up to us. But if we refuse to stop at a red light, we have lost sight of, or are rejecting, the ultimate project.

6.1 Democracy's parameters are its ultimate project. They imply the acceptance of certain limitations on actions: we may go to the church or temple of our choosing, but we may not compel others to do so too. Or: we may vote as we please, but we may not compel others to do so. Or: we may not kill those who disagree with us.

6.11 Because these parameters are largely accepted in stable democracies, the result is the freedom to emphasize differences as if they were not relative ones, but absolute. Each is allowed to vilify the other so long as the end result is only a vote or a judicial appointment.

People who fail to understand that this is only possible if we accept other things think it means there is nothing holding us together.

6.12 Democracy allows differing points of view within itself, but it has qualities as a whole. Some things must be agreed on, as we agree on rules for order in a meeting in which people may speak their minds. Democracy is like a traffic light.

Someone who rejects the parameters is not entitled to a voice within those parameters.

6.13 At the edge of greatest emphasis on differences within the parameters, there is no practical difference with emphasizing difference within the parameters, and challenging the parameters.

The temptation of those who hold their viewpoints as being more important than their adherence to the process will always be to burst the seams of the system.

6.14 Someone whose own religious belief required all others to believe the same, and who was willing to take steps to ensure that others did so, would by definition not be merely a player within the democratic game, but bent on its destruction. S/he would sense the stricture that s/he could worship as s/he chose but could not force others to do the same as a constraint. It might even be sensed as an insult to the religion, if that demands its own propagation.

Liberals vs. conservatives

6.2 We may call the two main camps within democracies liberal and conservative. Liberal and conservative, in addition to whatever else there is, constitute the world.

6.21 It's impossible to understand what characterizes each standpoint by trying to create coherence out of the tenets of what they support and reject. These seem without a pattern.

Liberals and conservatives both claim to be the guardian of "individualism," which each side understands in a different way. In the United States, each side claims to be the guardian of the Constitution.

Conservatives typically are in favor of capital punishment, killing people legally, but also of the "right to life" of every fetus. Conservatives are typically unconcerned with the death of enemy combatants, and accept of the death of our own soldiers (this is "the ultimate sacrifice"). Liberals typically favor "choice" in abortion but will not allow conservatives to similarly choose which version of teleology will be taught to students, Darwin's or that of the Bible.

6.22 Because there is no coherent pattern to differentiate the tenets of liberal from conservative, we often rely on the secondary qualities of lifestyle differences to differentiate them, or affiliation with one of the two major American parties if in the U.S. But the relationship between parties and their constituencies changes over time. This is the story of American politics.

6.23 Thus in order to see coherence in liberal and conservative agendas, we cannot merely list their tenets, nor can we identify them with one or the other of the two main political parties.

6.24 Each relies on an underlying deep-structural pattern which determines its nature.

When a liberal argues with a conservative, the argument is always about the surface level, because that is where disagreement is located. They will never achieve resolution, because they are disagreeing at the level made to permit disagreement.

At the deep-structure level there is no disagreement possible, only acknowledgement of differences. At the same time the deep-structural divergences are at least divergences on the same level, so that the two sides can continue to argue.

6.241 Argument presupposes sameness at some level. A cloud does not argue with a chair, nor a liberal with an aardvark.

Actions vs. actors

6.25 Both liberals and conservatives express their principles in terms of the social world. That is, in terms of ethics. Ethics is expressed in social terms. The individual always escapes ethics.

Conservatives express their dicta in terms of actions, liberals in terms of actors.

6.251 Conservative ethics postulates an action external to the actor, a rule that all people must follow, that the individual runs after. For this reason conservatives see themselves as self-sacrificing, dedicated to things larger than themselves. Liberal ethics starts with the person, which is to say the particular situation of the particular person.

6.252 A rule of the form "thou shalt not X" is a quintessentially conservative utterance, because it leaves no room to consider specifics of the "thou." Whoever "thou" is, s/he shall not X. X is unvarying.

Liberal thought will always try to look at the circumstances of the situation, because liberal thought expresses its ethical pronouncements in terms of actors. Liberal thought asks about the specifics of the actor: who was s/he? Why did s/he act? At this, conservatives snort in derision. It seems to them that liberals are trying to soften the blow, find a way to let the actor weasel out. The liberals see themselves as only trying to determine what happened.

6.2521 It's comical to hear a liberal and a conservative argue: the liberal thinks the conservative heartless, the conservative thinks the liberal weak and unfocused.

6.253 Conservative ethical thought is expressed in terms of units outside the individual that the individual must aspire to. The action pattern is always external to the individual, who must try to live up to it.

6.2531 It's difficult for liberal ethical thought to make pronouncements that are valid for all situations, and extremely easy for conservative thought. This produces conservative impatience with liberals.

The closest liberal thought has ever come up with to an absolute ethical stricture is the Golden Rule. Its rule is a non-rule, making what to do dependent on individual circumstances.

Conservatives do not like the Golden Rule. Liberals do.

6.254 Because the actor is always secondary to the action in conservative thought, any divergence between actor and action is something the actor is responsible for.

Conservatives pride themselves on the "tough love" this produces. It does so because conservative thought simply does not operate at the level of individual variations. If the only alternative to the individual is the action, then of course the individual is responsible.

6.2541 This leads to the fact that conservatives are more willing to punish transgressions than liberals, or (typically) to kill others in battle. The phrase "compassionate conservative" makes clear that normally conservatism will always rule against the individual. Only unearned mercy can temper justice.

6.2542 This is the reason for conservative love of the smiting hand of Yahweh of the Hebrew Bible ("Old Testament") and their frequent adoption of the language of the King James Bible in everyday conversation. Renaissance English sounds agreeably old-fashioned and so, compared to our brief lives, eternal. If they were living in the sixteenth century, they would presumably have to speak Latin to get the same feeling. If in the Roman Empire, perhaps Aramaic.

6.255 Conservatives enjoy making fun of the liberal desire to talk with malefactors, convince them they were wrong.

Conservatives pride themselves on their toughness: blow them away. But this is not because of a belief that people beyond the pale cannot be reasoned with. If this were primary, they would not be contemptuous of the liberal attempt to do so, but would argue against it (unless their method is to blow away liberals as well). Instead, the idea seems to conservatives not wrong but ridiculous, not on their map.

The quintessential conservative reaction is the snort of derision: How ridiculous. And they turn away.

Liberals, by contrast, are always ready to show you how wrong you are. They want to interact with the individual.

6.26 At their worst, conservatives are bulls in a china shop, flailing about in the name of doing something, anything. They fail to consider the consequences, or are contemptuous of those who do.

At *their* worst, liberals are Hamlets, afraid to take a bold stroke because they are unable to say for sure what the consequences will be.

6.27 The military, based on action rather than thought, as well as on physical power, is an intrinsically conservative calling.

Conservatives like the structure of the military as well as what it does. For conservatives, the best is an absolute rule. Second best is one person deciding absolutely. All institutions are hierarchical, so all institutions, as institutions, are by nature conservative.

Don't Do It

6.3 Expressing rules in terms of actions, not actors, means that they are valid for everyone, no matter who we are. This leads to what seems to liberals an absolutist slant to conservative thought. For liberals, conservatives are proto-fascists.

This is not the way conservatives see themselves. For conservatives the point is not adherence to the collective, the core of fascism, but each person's adherence to the absolute external Rule. Thus conservatives are not harder on themselves than they are on others. This lets conservatives see themselves as rough and tough, but fair.

6.301 The conservative viewpoint jibes to a great degree with the male viewpoint. It emphasizes things we can control, which means things within our immediate ken. (The further away things become the less we think we can control them.) It emphasizes action rather than thought.

6.31 The difference between the structure of liberal and conservative thought is summed up in a taunting liberal bumper sticker. "Don't Believe in Abortion? Don't Do It." Liberals know that conservatives not only want themselves not to perform abortions, but for no one to perform abortions. What liberals want, however, is for the people who want to perform abortions to perform abortions, and the people who don't, not to. They know that if this understanding is adopted, they have carried the day.

6.32 From a liberal point of view, conservative thought is intrinsically geared towards everyone doing the same thing.

In fact it is geared toward seeing the world in terms of action, which simply fails to touch the question of actors involved in it. This seems a fine distinction, but one that drives both liberals and conservatives to each others' throats.

Liberals compare conservatives to absolutist religious regimes, fundamentalist Christianity to fundamentalist Islam. Conservatives do not like the comparison. This is because non-believers conceive of religions from the outside. Conservatives conceive of themselves as running after rules of action, trying to attain them.

6.33 The structure of limitation that is democracy is, as overstructure, closer to the liberal point of view than to the conservative.

The vision of many opinions being allowed to fight so that no one opinion predominates, central to the Federalist Papers, is a liberal notion.[61]

6.331 The point of view of the individuals fighting is closer to the conservative.

6.332 Both points of view are necessary in the system. Within a democracy, liberal and conservative are as linked by these differences as they are separated.

6.34 Opinions vary regarding the ways all participants in the democratic process should acknowledge the framework.

Because conservative thought is expressed in terms of actions, patriotism for conservatives is expressed in actions undertaken by the system as a whole with respect to what is outside it. Conservatives identify patriotism with fighting enemies.

Liberals do not define patriotism in terms of actions against the outside, but in terms of what is allowed inside. This is usually called tolerance.

6.341 To conservatives, this seems insufficiently active, even effeminate.

6.342 The conservative position is closer to a tragic sense of life: people really aren't that important. This is why conservative thought links so well with all kinds of religion, which typically emphasize the vanity of human wishes.

This is the lure to world-weary intellectuals of conservative ethics. The Modernists provided many examples: T. S. Eliot, W. B. Yeats, Ezra Pound.

Sex

6.4 One of the subjects that polarizes liberals and conservatives very quickly is sex and the subjects related to it: abortion, pornography, marriage. The arguments are foreseeable in all cases. This so because of the nature of sexuality and the nature of the liberal/conservative divide.

6.41 Sex is intrinsically problematic.

6.42 Sex makes us uncomfortable because it belongs neither to the private nor to the public realm, the two clearly defined realms of our lives, but partly to both. It is more public than private things and more private than public.

Those completely in the private realm—those afraid to be touched, intensely private people—avoid sex. Those who live completely in the public realm avoid sex: there's neither time nor place for it that's not full of interactions with other people, sound and motion.

6.43 We must find sex partners initially in the public realm, but sex acts take us away from the public realm into a more personal one, shared with another person.

6.431 Initially we must act in a very social, codified way with other people. The deeper we get into a sexual relationship, the more we're making things up as we go along into things that aren't codified. We leave the social world. This means, we leave the codifiable world. Our relationship becomes *sui generis*, one of a kind.

The French express this strange combination of personal and private neatly by calling a passionate love affair a *folie à deux*, a shared delusion. We see things the way the other person does, but both of us together diverge from the rest of the world.

6.44 Ethics is the language of the social realm, general rules. Individual occurrences don't enter the world of rules, unless they are re-defined as not being individual at all. Thus it is the social realm that hunts down sexuality as miscegenation between two realms.

Things clearly beyond the power of ethics, completely in the personal realm, escape the ire of ethics. It is only mixed, half and half things, of which sex is the most widespread example, that causes ethics to see red.

6.441 Both liberal and conservative ethics try to hunt down sex. Conservative ethics rejects the non-social aspect of sex: it is seen as self-gratifying. Liberal ethics sees sex as unfair to the subordinate partner. Feminist theory that rejects male-female sex for the position it puts women in expresses the liberal position.

6.45 Our collective sense of the half-way nature of sexuality is expressed by our embarrassment in talking about the sexual realm with others.

6.451 The explanation religion offers for why we are embarrassed by sexuality is part of a larger story that over time ceased to seem plausible for many people. The story involved Adam and Eve's actions as part of a larger fore-ordained pattern of sin and redemption.

6.4511 Freud felt obliged to offer a secular explanation for this phenomenon.[62]

He thought society as a whole drove sexuality underground because not doing so would destroy the society. The result of driving so much raw power underground was highly developed civilization, which worked off the energy produced by the confinement of this power. We are taught to be leery of bringing sexuality into the open. The result is embarrassment.

Freud's interest was in providing a scientific explanation of the individual. Thus his explanation was of necessity undifferentiated with respect to individuals. In this sense it is a conservative theory.

6.4512 Freud painted with too broad a brush. The reason we're embarrassed by sex is not the nature of society as a whole. The proof of this is that sometimes we're not embarrassed by sex at all, and there are times and places where sexuality isn't repressed, kept underground.

6.452 Society admits of many gradations of the social. It's the intensely social that is the enemy of sexuality, not society as a whole.

This is so because focus on collective projects is more intense.

6.4521 Sexuality creates bubbles within the social world that are inaccessible to it, private worlds.

6.4522 In certain circumstances we must be completely social beings. This means, absolutely predictable. Sexual relationships are not predictable. To a large degree, we make them up as we go along. To a large degree they escape the social sphere.

Those societies or sub-groups that discourage or condemn sexuality are those where the individual is turned completely inside out to the group. The projects people are following are collective, and people must stay focused on them all the time.

In the military people speak again and again of "the mission," and on "staying focused." There's no time to form unpredictable semi-personal bubbles of sexual relationships. In the Navy the order or priority is: ship, shipmate, self.

6.453 There are other situations in society where we wish to keep others on a very short leash, be able to predict their actions. One is parenting, where the parents feel responsible for virtually all their children do. Raising the children is their long-term project, that which determines many other smaller projects. In order to help the children, they must be aware of practically everything going on in and with the child. This is the reason we insist that children, or subordinates in the military, not lie to us. The result is that parents typically don't encourage their children's sexuality and are sometimes very embarrassed even to talk about it. Fathers deal worst of all with their daughters', because fathers are taught to be responsible for their daughters in a way they are not with the sons, who are typically acknowledged to be independent entities at an earlier age.

We accept the sexuality of adult children, if we do, not because they are adults, but because we no longer feel responsible for them, which we express by saying they are adults.

6.4531 Similarly children, who see their parents as existing only or primarily for them, typically do not want to think of their parents as sexual beings.

6.454 The intense socialization of childhood is a result of the young age of children. The intense socialization of the military is the result of a temporary situation. In both cases we treat the people whose sexuality we are intolerant of as less than equals. This is another way of saying, we are responsible for them.

We are not responsible for equals.

Either we are responsible for someone or to someone, or we are free to go off the beaten path in the sideways of individual sexuality. If Freud were right, we wouldn't have this choice.

6.46 It would seem that the personal world would be tolerated even less well in these intensely social situations than the mixed one of sexuality, being further yet from the social. But this is not the case. The personal world is put on hold but not hunted down. It is sufficiently far as to be clearly different, and so poses no category threat. Officers in a submarine may be roused by duty from sleep at any time, but they are allowed to sleep. On their time off they sit around the ward room. The personal is acknowledged as something different, even if it is kept within bounds.

It is sexuality, that near-social thing, that raises the ire of those focused tightly on projects. Sex is forbidden on mixed-sex ships (it is not addressed on all-male boats as submarines in the U.S. Navy currently are, being assumed to be non-existent). Of course forbidding it on aircraft carriers, where men and women serve together, doesn't mean it doesn't happen. (See 6.44.)

If we need to have 24/7 access to other people, allowing them to have sex makes this access impossible. So we forbid the sex.

Pornography

6.461 We are almost always more annoyed by positions closer to ours than by those further away. We feel at least we are fighting over the same territory. Things further away are simply too remote.

6.462 This is the reason pornography is so fought over. To those in the ethical realm, the social realm, pornography is infuriating. At first glance this seems strange, as so much of the consumption of pornography is in the personal realm. But it's not totally personal. It requires props, and it takes up room. It exists in the social realm.

The consumption of pornography is part of a spectrum of sexual actions more personal than actual intercourse, that become increasingly more personal as they move toward fantasy, and increasingly more social as they move toward action.

Fantasy is almost completely beyond the reach of the ethical (social) realm, being almost completely individual. Only a God who knows our thoughts can impose ethics on fantasy, as for example in the Christian concept of "committing adultery in our heart." Sexual fantasy is both further away from and less annoying to ethics than pornography is.

Sexual actions are social enough that ethics is full of strictures about them. Real sex is less infuriating to ethics than pornography is because ethics can get a better purchase on it.

6.4621 Frequently ethical thinkers try to link pornography to actions in the social realm as a way of expressing their disapproval. Their claim is that this is what makes it illegitimate (e.g. reading about bondage and domination makes people engage in these actions).

But pornography is precisely that thing that teeters between the personal and the social realm, and any connections with action will always be only in specific cases. We'll never be able to say what the general effects of consuming pornography are any more than we can say what the general effects of consuming novels is. (Does reading *Madame Bovary* encourage women to be adulteresses, or discourage them?[63])

6.46211 Because art is not communication and always dabbles in the world off to the side of our projects, it is problematic in something of the same way as pornography, or sexuality in general.

6.4622 One objection to pornography does not hinge on claims to its effects in the social realm. That is, that it gives "air time" to things those objecting disapprove of. It makes them more real. They *are* to a greater degree than before. (This is not the same as saying, people are more likely to emulate these practices subsequently.)

Casanova

6.47 If we need not pursue commonly held projects, our margin to indulge our sexuality widens exponentially.

Those people with the luxury or ability to avoid the projects that define most other people's lives will have no trouble expressing their sexuality. The Marquis de Sade had no trouble expressing his sexuality, nor Casanova. It's not coincidence that neither had to work for a living. The pursuit of sexuality became their project. Casanova had such success with women because the husbands were typically off doing manly things in the world. This left the boudoir to him.

The price for this ability to express themselves in these strange semi-personal relationships was that these men had few of the kind of relationships on short leashes that typify relationships with family or the military.

6.48 We can't both doggedly pursue projects and explore to a great degree in the to-be-invented byways of sexuality. One takes us forward; the other goes sideways.

6.5 Ethics will always try to limit sexuality to the predictable. This is so not because ethics has a will of its own but because this is the nature of its structure and vocabulary.

There is no way to make sexuality completely predictable, because of its nature. Part of it is always sticking out into the private realm, where ethics cannot tread.

6.51 Only when personal things can be expressed in social terms do they enter ethics. Ethics has no view whether I should choose vanilla or chocolate ice cream. We can see no possible link of this choice to others. But it may have a view on whether vanilla beans should be harvested in the rain forest, because we can see a link between this and the social realm.

6.52 Pursuing sexuality may mean accepting that we are acting outside of the purview of ethics. That is, in the unseen part of the iceberg.

6.53 Conservative thought, drawing on writings by Sts. Augustine and Thomas, provides a purpose for sex.[64] This is quintessential conservative thought, giving the rule for action.

6.531 Liberal thought, by contrast, will tend to find out what something, in this case sex, can be used for. What are its effects? is a liberal question.

6.532 Marriage, a social institution, draws a fence around sexuality and lets us ignore what is going on inside. As St. Paul put it, "it is better to marry than to burn (with lust)."[65] Best of all, he said, would be to adopt his own celibacy.

If marriage didn't exist, ethics would have to invent it.

6.5321 There is no intrinsic link between marriage and sex. Marriage tends to work against sex at least to some degree, in what we call "bed death." Many men have felt a tension between their desire to couple with many women and the demands of marriage for monogamy. Some women have felt this too.

Abortion

6.6 Abortion seems horrible to conservatives. If the purpose of intercourse is children, and we prevent this from happening, we are at complete counter-purposes to the universe.

6.61 Liberals do not accept this notion of being at counter-purposes to the universe. If I can do it, then it's possible. I'm part of the universe. As always, this starts with the actor, not the action.

In conservative thought, it is perfectly possible for an individual to be at counter-purposes to the universe, because action is primary and the actor secondary. In liberal thought, the individual is primary, so is a contradiction in terms to speak of being at counter-purposes to the universe. We add up the individuals: that is the universe. For this reason it is conservatives who vilify homosexuality as being "against nature."

6.611 Nor, according to conservatives, may we *sometimes* have abortions for reasons X, Y, and Z. If the purpose of sex is having children, then individual circumstances are irrelevant to the fundamental necessity to have children.

6.62 Conservatives appear to be very interested in the birth of this particular child. ("It's a child, not a choice.")

6.621 In fact, conservative thought is interested in children (in general), but not in this particular child, or any particular child. To be so would be to think in a way incommensurate with conservative thought.

6.622 Each child conceived "kills" (prevents from being born) the myriad of other children that could have been conceived if another sperm had reached the egg first, and during the ensuring nine months plus a few months.

If conservative thought were interested in *this* child being born or not being born, it would have to be equally interested in these other unborn children, the ones that might have been. What is the value of *this* child as opposed to the others it displaces? They never get to be alive to speak for themselves.

In fact conservative thought does not think of these possibilities at all. It states its belief that "life begins at conception."

Why conception when so many zygotes fail to implant properly and so are "aborted" naturally? Why not say, life begins on a trial basis at a live birth, whenever that is, and becomes stronger the longer the infant survives?

Why pick conception, other than that's what's picked?

This kind of sliding scale of life is foreign to the conservative need to have clear lines and absolutes of action.

6.6221 Conservative thought with respect to abortion is victor's justice. The people who were born were meant to be born. So suggesting that they could have been aborted seems an affront not only to this individual but somehow to God's plan.

Yet of course we don't know about the ones that didn't implant properly in the mother. Or was it God's plan for these not to make it?

6.622 Nor is there anything particularly inevitable about me. If I had not been born, my parents would undoubtedly have had another child in my stead, someone else.

Or is it clearly not God's will that that should have happened, given that it didn't? What is, is. This much is clear.

6.6223 If anything that happens is God's will, why isn't deciding not to have this child now in favor of one later (producing a voluntary abortion) God's will as well?

6.6224 At the same time conservatives frequently argue against, say, gay marriages producing children: it's better for children to have two parents, one of each sex.

Perhaps this is so, but if *this* child was meant to be born, it was better that it be born to two lesbians with the aid of a sperm donor than not be born at all.

Apparently this is the child that was meant to be born.

It's not as if the same child could have been born to a heterosexual couple. That already would have made it different, these circumstances.

6.623 Liberals take the perspective that is congruent with that of the mother. This is the reason liberal thought has been adopted by women seeking "control of their own bodies."

The mother knows the time before the child, perhaps remembering the decision to try and conceive it. Thus the mother *does* compare the conceived child with unconceived children. The child that is surges as if by chance from a cloud of possibles.

For conservatives, the fetus is an "unborn child." Conservatives eliminate the cloud of possibles, and start with the child that is. They do not admit gradations of possible: it is, or it isn't.

6.624 Conservatives emphasize the extent to which the unborn child is like a person. That is the category they have put it in. Thus the discovery that DNA is identical in a one-day old zygote and the old (wo)man it may some day become is grist for their mill. But they seize on this fact because they want to emphasize the identical nature of this creature with an adult. It could still be true and not prove what they want it to prove.

So many other things, after all, are different.

6.625 The deep structure of conservative thought produces the conservative tendency to think of the woman's body as a passive vessel, a kind of conduit through which the human being must pass on its journey into the world.

If this really were so, and the woman completely passive, they wouldn't have to enjoin women not to interrupt this journey. It wouldn't be interruptable.

6.6251 Conservative thought is obliged to argue that gestation is a slippery slope, something that must, once started at point A, end at point Z. Of course they know it needn't.

They see gestation as what I call a "hard process."

In order to survive, zygotes must not only form, but implant properly, then move to the next stage successfully, and the next, and the next. And this blurs what for conservatives is the clear distinction between state A, non-existence (pre-conception) and state B, a healthy college graduate ready to face the world. Conservative thought must by definition demote to secondary status all of the hurdles that must be surmounted along the way in order to justify their binary definition of person/not person.

6.62511 Similarly the work of hospitals and teams of doctors, technology, and money, necessary to keeping a prematurely born child alive is waved away by conservatives. This isn't what made the child a person. It merely preserved what was meant to be.

How do we know this? Because the end result was, the child was saved.

If the child was not saved, the person, for reasons we cannot access, died. Medicine, like the mother, is a passive thing. Neither actually contributes anything, according to conservatives.

6.6252 Our notion of what constitutes a hard process can change. In the early years of the Common Era illness was thought to be a hard process. It was interfering with God to attempt a cure; we could only pray that He lift the illness.[66]

Nowadays we do not regard illness as a hard process. Instead health is postulated; illness is a negative that may be removed.

6.626 Conservative thought attempts to push its reach back to what for it is the earliest possible moment, conception.

But why stop there? It's only science that got us to conception; perhaps it can get us yet further back. In the eighteenth century, the earliest we could think of the baby as a being was birth. Now, with ultrasound and electron microscopes, we can see further back than birth, so to with care for the prematurely born. Perhaps someday science will identify the pheromones that draw together the parents. Should the first meeting of the parents not be thought of as the true beginning of this person? Even now, we can as defensibly argue that the child that ultimately arrives exists on the wedding day as we can argue that it exists as a zygote. This is an arbitrarily chosen point in time.

6.6261 Religious conservatives speak of "ensoulment," the moment at which the soul enters the child to be born. By definition this can never be proven or justified to someone who questions it. Nor can conservatives justify their claim that it happens at conception. That's what they believe.

6.627 Currently, we tend to regard "belief" as a kind of protection against others that works like using garlic against vampires. It's supposed to keep others at bay. As in: I believe that life starts at conception. Back off. Or: I believe that marriage is between a man and a woman. And the conversation is supposed to stop.

Yet only within the group does "belief" function as an end to conversation. Outside the group it only signals that we may ask for explanation.

6.63 Conservative thought is strongest in saying that its practitioners "choose life." They mean, having children rather than not having children. Because conservative thought is expressed in terms of actions, conservative ethics cannot fine-tune actions to the situations of particular actors. The choices are: have baby (babies) or don't have baby (babies). Not: have baby X later rather than baby Y now, or if our financial situation improves, or if I meet a woman I get along better with than this one.

6.631 Conservative thought does not compare this baby with another possible baby, one situation with another situation, only the abstract completely unspecific act of "having baby" with "not having baby."

Who would choose that no one had babies? In this sense, everyone would choose life.

6.632 But liberals could (and do) say, for example, they don't want to have a baby now, but later. They will allow one of the millions of other possible babies which is prevented from coming to be because the mother's womb is taken over by the fetus that is there already to come to be.

Or they might say: other people have enough babies for all, so why should they?

6.633 When conservatives object to birth control, it's because this is being compared to never having children, not to having children at another time: this is the only way it can be expressed in terms of actions, rather than of actors. Rules, the language of conservative thought, are blind to the individual people they affect or the individual situation they're used in.

6.64 When it seems conservative thought is being dictatorial and doctrinaire, it is in fact only applying the only kind of rule it allows, those in terms of actions. This means: no fine tuning according to individuals. The action is always the action. Doing it once for conservatives implies doing it always.

6.641 This is the aspect of conservative thought that alienates many intellectuals.

Those intellectuals who do end up being conservatives come to this as a kind of security net after being overwhelmed by an ethics requiring fine-tuning to situations. It is the anti-intellectual aspect of conservative thought that appeals to world-weary liberals, who then become conservatives.

6.65 To liberals, conservatives seem unrealistic. We do make distinctions in life. Now may not be the same as later.

6.651 Similarly, liberals reject the conservative insistence that an action can have only one (primary) purpose, and we know what it is. Liberals say: even if we can acknowledge that the (main) purpose of eating is in fact to keep us alive, not everything we eat has to be what keeps us alive, even though it is certainly true that if we do not eat anything, we will die. Thus some sex is procreative, but much isn't. Some needs to result in babies, but not all. Similarly, liberals might say: Some pregnancies need to result in babies, but not all.

Liberal thought allows description of the situation in more individual terms, because that is the nature of liberal thought.

6.66 Beings on both ends of the normal spectrum of "people" transcend the boundaries of usual language. Even if we speak, in the manner of conservatives, of an "unborn child" rather than a fetus, this implies that we can say of this creature, that in some fundamental sense is not yet, what it is.

The liberal may well reason as follows: If this being is most fundamentally a person, then what are its likes and dislikes? Its personality traits?

The person most like the unborn child is, unsurprisingly, the just-born child, where we see the shape of a human being but have no sense of the person's personality.

6.661 Not-yet-people are comparable in vocabulary to once-were people. We don't really know how to talk about them. Many people use the same word for both of these two groups, "soul," but no one really knows what this means.

This is because it is a thing whose nature is precisely to provide the continuity between a person and a once-was person. That is its only sure quality.

6.6611 Let's say we accept that we live on after death (once-were people) as angels. But if we have no sex as angels, no need to remember our favorite music, no need to tell others about how much we loved to go to New York, no need of our life partners, no age (unless we accept that everybody is 33, like Jesus at His death—do we have tooth-wear patterns of 33-year-olds? But we have better dental hygiene nowadays), and perhaps even no size (how many angels can dance on the head of a pin?), then in what sense are they us? Do they have consciousness of our particular pasts? How odd to think that our eternal soul should be sitting on a cloud thinking of, say, pepperoni pizza.

6.6612 Similarly, we might wonder, in what sense is a zygote like us? It doesn't see (no eyes), feel, like red wine, or root for the Dodgers. It just sits there, two cells multiplying.

If it does this enough, it can become us. But why say it is so now?

Purpose of sex

6.7 For conservatives, the purpose of sex is the production of children, and always in marriage. This is the effect of sex that most completely re-integrates it into the social realm, which is the happy hunting ground of ethics.

6.71 They almost always make the logically independent assertion that other forms of sex are illegitimate.

6.72 Voltaire makes fun of conservative thinking in *Candide* when he has the butt of his jokes, Dr. Pangloss, opine that noses were made to put spectacles on; we know this because they do carry spectacles. Legs were made to wear trousers. We know this because they do so.[67] Sexual intercourse has as its only visible physical effect the production of children, so for conservatives, this is clearly the purpose. Purpose is understood as: the *only* purpose.

Pangloss is ridiculous because he has fastened on only one, much subsequent effect and proclaimed this the purpose. We're willing to say that people existed so long before glasses we can't tie glasses to noses intrinsically.

But who says we have to identify a single purpose to begin with? Why not merely a growing list of uses, or effects? In order to pick one, we must justify this choice not as our own individual choice, but as part of a collective belief system. (See 4.7.)

Religion tells us what the purpose of X is, we can't intuit it or figure it out. We can't justify our belief that it the purpose of X is Y by saying, this is my personal belief, only by saying, this is what belief system Z says.

6.73 The liberal will point out that intercourse fails to produce a child more often than not, and that what most people are conscious of is the pleasure involved. Why can't this pleasure be "the" purpose, or at least "a" purpose? Why do we have to think in terms of purpose at all?

Some hint of accepting the notion that sex may have more than one purpose (though of course one remains primary) seems behind the Church's allowance of a "unitive" function to married sex.[68]

The notion that the "purpose" of sex is the production of children works better, in any case, with the man than with the woman. The male orgasm is normally accompanied by ejaculation of semen. For the woman, whose orgasm is independent of ovulation, such a notion is only defensible if we express the purpose in the long run. Seeking orgasm, the argument will run, the women, sooner or later, conceives.

But by this point the correlation seems too far removed from the individual case, almost as silly as Pangloss's saying that the purpose of noses is to hold up spectacles.

6.731 What is the purpose of eating? We do not currently fight over whether this is to stay alive. We accept that this is the effect, and revel in the different tastes we can get from this animalistic process. We do not demand that everything we put in our mouths be part of this project of staying alive.

6.732 Many of what liberals call "inconsistencies" of the conservative position are in fact not so. They are the result of the structure of conservative thought, which expresses its tenets in terms of absolute rules for action. So long as we do these actions, many things are in a neutral zone. It's liberals who see the individual case and ask, what about these actions?

6.733 If it has been determined that the woman is fertile for only a few days a month, and procreation is the purpose, then conservative thought has by definition no opinion about intercourse during the non-fertile period. It is not inconsistent for conservatives not to comment on the fact that sex during this period apparently has as its function something other than the production of children (pleasure?). For them, this period is secondary.

Not conceiving during most of the month is thus radically different from preventing conception during the fertile time. This is usually expressed as acting "against nature." It presupposes that we accept we know what the purpose of this action is.

6.734 It is not a contradiction for conservatives to accept marriages that, for reasons beyond the control of the individuals, do not or cannot result in conception, such as marriage of old people, or sterile people. These at least have the forms of marriages, in some sense "do honor" to marriages that can produce children.

Here as always, whatever we have decided to be the purpose of an action automatically relegates to a secondary level any action that does not contribute to the carrying out of this purpose.

6.735 To conservatives, liberals seem presumptuous. Conservatives are much more willing to simply "let go and let God." But at the same time, according to conservative thought, people may not actively thwart the one thing determined to be the purpose. By contrast to the laws, people are quite unimportant. Conservatives express this by speaking in terms of the action: the action may not be undertaken (by anyone).

6.74 Conservatives will always choose the most social definition of purpose available. Thus conservative thought, in an effort to codify and make sexuality social, could not ever determine that the purpose of sex is pleasure. This is an individual state. For liberals, conservatives are always killjoys. In fact, they are simply trying to codify in terms of rules for action.

Cavemen did it

6.8 One of the most interesting arguments used to justify a claim that "the purpose of sex is procreation" is that we modern people should do the things our cavemen ancestors did. These arguments are called bio-evolutionary. What we do, X, is "the same" as what cavemen did, therefore it's essential to our continued existence, therefore we should do X (and not Y).

Usually the real point for this argument is the (and not Y).

Sometimes the real argument is: in fact we're *not* doing X, and should be, since the cavemen did.

6.81 To get even one instance of continuity, we have to phrase what we do so as to create that continuity. Bio-evolutionary arguments are circular. They are all attempts to give a secular version of religious arguments regarding fundamental purpose.

6.82 We tailor the articulation of what we want to justify to allow us to say we are doing the "same" thing as our cavemen ancestors. We make the link to our ancestors by knowing (at least so we believe) what they did, and saying that what we do is the "same." However without independent knowledge of cavemen we could never get from what we do to a description of what they had to have done.

We don't say: playing Nintendo and wearing cotton shirts keeps the species going. Only something along the lines of: playing and being clothed. We strip away the particulars to aim at establishing a commonality we have in fact already assumed.

6.83 We pick and choose what we focus on, what we want to justify by linking it to the past. Nobody says that cutting our hair short contributes to the longevity of mankind. So apparently we can do new things without it endangering the species. Or is it simply going to take a while for its nefarious effects to be clear? Or do we simply say we don't know if it's a species-preserving thing or no?

6.831 The idea is that if something we do is what our ancestors did (have sex, eat, clothe ourselves, and so on), has to promote the survival of the species.

6.84 No one ever said that evolution was the most efficient possible process, only that it made efficient choices (those pointing to survival) when given such choices. Thus we may be rife with qualities that do not lead to survival, or even those that work against it. It's just that situations have not placed these against other qualities that would have been even better for us, or that we have been strong enough to take the hits offered by negative behavior. So the fact that we've always done something doesn't end up showing it contributed to species longevity either.

6.841 We probably wouldn't visualize our forebears as being those in the court of Marie Antoinette. A few hundred years isn't enough to produce the winnowing we are presupposing. But who says a few tens of thousands are enough to winnow everything? Are we at the apogee of development?

6.85 If evolution works as a cumulative force, we don't have to try as individuals to promote the survival of the species. If it is true, it tells what is going to happen. We don't have to help it happen.

6.86 Because such arguments are always conservative (do the *same* thing), they always express the action as an absolute, presupposing that the choice is 100% this or 100% not-this. Sometimes people say, for example, practice X (say, abortion or homosexuality) can't be pro-evolutionary, because if practiced by everyone, it would cause the death of the species. But evolution may be perfectly happy with enough of what it has to continue the species. The rest may be irrelevant.

Being heterosexual

6.87 Men tend to care more than women do whether other men are heterosexual.

If we accept the widely-held view that heterosexuality is defined by "object choice," this fact seems puzzling.[69] Two men with different "types" in women will never compete. Why should they care that both of their "types" are part of a larger category of "women"? Yet most men do seem to care, intensely, about being sure that other men take women as their sexual objects.

But the point isn't that the men are taking women. It's that the men aren't taking men. Heterosexuality is defined with respect to men, not with respect to women. It's the object not chosen, not the object chosen, that counts.

6.871 Men like to be in control of the sexual situation. They like to be assured that the men they associate with will not try to approach them. Or that other men, whom they treat as versions of themselves, do not permit themselves to be penetrated. They want to be able to look at someone and know that he's not a possible sexual partner, and that he is to be treated as an equal. Things are clear that way.

6.872 Most descriptions of heterosexuality, influenced by Foucault, have come from a point of view outside heterosexuality.[70] From without, heterosexuality seems to be the power position, straight men obsessed with retaining their dominance.

From within, heterosexuality is quite different than this, much less substantial. Being a man is a goal, a thing achieved. It's something every heterosexual man is running after. Sometimes he catches it, sometimes he doesn't.

As a result, heterosexual men do not understand definitions of heterosexuality from without that see straight men as power-mad oppressors. What? they say. Us the oppressors? We're too busy getting it up and keeping it up.

6.8721 Masculinity is something that must be achieved. Straight men rise to challenges, and test their own masculinity based on whether or not they do so.

It annoys straight men when outsiders—women, gay men—assume that the achievement of this so-precarious state can be taken for granted. What the straight man mostly feels is his own insufficiency, or relief that this time, he need not feel insufficient. But what about next?

Men are always trying to live up to their balls, to shoulder the burdens associated with being male. This means, both with respect to men, and with respect to women. Being a male means taking on a place in a position of relationships.

6.873 To the straight man, being heterosexual isn't an essence, it's a series of actions. This is exactly the opposite of the Foucauldian claim, which is an outsider's viewpoint.

6.8731 Life is a series of challenges that a man must meet.

6.8732 With old age they fail to be met more and more frequently.

6.8733 Old age for men is ignominious in a way that old age for women is not. A "little old lady" is sweet. A "little old man" is, unfortunately, contemptible, at least for men who are neither little nor old.

6.88 Straight men typically fail to see other men in sexual terms because they put these creatures in a certain category. Not the reverse.

6.881 In a similar way, men put some women in the category of "cannot even be considered as a sex object": daughters, mothers, the female boss. But everyone has felt a person abruptly change place from this category to the "can be considered as a sex object" category: a long-time friend whom suddenly we see as a possible romantic interest, for example.

6.881 The world can be set on its ear if one day a man suddenly does see a member of one of the categories "that way." The shift is instantaneous. The other person is otherwise unchanged; the man merely sees the other person differently. Say, he sees his daughter's best friend in a sexual manner. More horrifyingly, his daughter.

The attraction is determined not by what the person looks like, but by what power configuration the person is in with respect to him or her.

6.882 A good deal of being straight with other straight men consists of things that are the case but that cannot be said. If you acknowledge certain things about yourself, you lose the advantage you want to keep over other men. You lose power. Keeping the power position is precisely the balancing act of straightness.

6.883 Not saying to other men many of the things that we could say is merely a definition of being straight, not a proof that it is something else. And not saying means, most of the time, not even thinking them.

Thought is largely habitual. It takes on its own projects.

6.884 Not saying to a degree ensures not saying. Because it isn't an option, we don't think about it, with men or women.

Sex and power

6.9 Why do some men who have sex with women want to be tied up by them? Why do some like pinning down women and ramming into them? Why do some men who have sex with other men want to be on the top? Why do some want to be on the bottom? Why do some women choose to be with women for their college years and then marry men?

6.91 A more flexible measure of sexual expression than merely "being straight" or "being gay" is required if we accept all these things as needing explanation as much as "why are all objects of my desire female?"

6.92 A more flexible yard stick is the one calibrated in terms of power.

6.921 All relations with others, whether sexual, non-sexual, or anywhere in between, are relations on a scale whose calibration is in terms of power.

The fact that are relations are measured in terms of power is the reason others are so horrified when, instead of protecting the people we are supposed to protect, we approach them sexually. We aren't supposed to interact in that way with our daughters or our female students.

6.923 Desire flows in the conduits created by power relations for its passage. If suddenly a blockage is removed, we can be bowled over by the force of its re-direction.

6.924 Other beings on the same level in the power grid are similarly unavailable for lopsided power relations. Usually this means, other men. It can also mean, a co-worker. Certainly it means the female boss. This leaves only certain women.

6.925 Biology has assigned men and women default roles in this power play because of the construction of sex organs (what makes us speak of "male-female" joints in plumbing) and the typically greater strength of the male. These defaults act like the obvious positions (say, quarter-hours) on an analogue watch dial. We can feel the hands "tending" to these places.

6.9251 Thus while we acknowledge the drift, like a tide taking us in a certain direction, we can use this as something to play with. We can act at cross-purposes to these roles, or suspend them temporarily, as we can set watch hands just "off" the obvious, or against this position. Working against these magnet points, this default, is also working with it.

6.9252 The difference between sex (biological body) and gender (the role we play) is shown in the fact that women can play this dominant role too, with men or with other women. Most women will probably not want to do this most of the time, but some may. Most men will like being the one in charge, but some may not, and even those who normally do may not all the time.

6.9253 Many current thinkers have assumed that because it is possible to separate sex from gender theoretically, that there is no correlation between them. This isn't true, and certainly can't be assumed. Why don't we drop the theory and ask how people interact?

6.9254 There is enough individual variation between people that we may simply have to ask, at the appropriate moment: what do you like to do?

Unless people have thought about just this question and have some experience, they are unlikely to know the answer.

6.93 We acknowledge these fundamental polarities by the way our daily language uses sexual terminology to indicate getting the upper hand, or losing it: I was fucked, I was screwed.

6.931 Penetration gives the upper hand to the penetrator. The upper hand, itself a metaphor, is here symbolic. "Blow me," a male says dismissively to another male. Or: "Suck my dick." Usually this means, I know you would never suck my dick, and I insult you by pretending I can order you to do so. (The issue is not wanting, but doing.) When a presumably straight male says in exasperation, "well, fuck me," this means: I am so stupid I deserve to be penetrated.

6.932 Men must enjoy the power position to be sexually attractive to most women.

Men who are at ease with their own bodies and with themselves are for that reason attractive to women. Men who are overly concerned with their looks and seem self-conscious are generally not attractive to women.

6.9321 This is the basis of the gender asymmetry producing the generalization that men do the looking, women are the looked-at. Sometimes it's fun for men to be the looked-at, and the women to be the lookers.

6.9322 Traditional (conservative) societies have tended to put labels on people. Women are the subservient sex in the bedroom has been held to imply they are the subservient sex in other aspects of life. Modern society leaves women similarly adrift: given power out of the bedroom, they may not realize they have to relinquish it in the bedroom if they wish to have sex with men. It is easier to be one person all the time, dominant or submissive. But if we learn the markers for changing positions, it can be done: a woman takes down her hair and puts on a "little black dress." All it takes is some flexibility.

6.9323 Saying that women are typically the ones dominated in sex with a man is true, but it determines nothing about the rest of the day or about how they are to be treated in other situations. If sex takes up a half an hour a day, then the other 23 ½ hours remain to be determined. If a man and a woman are not sexually involved, the undetermined time is 24 hours.

6.933 Liberal ethics disapproves of male-female sexuality because of the natural givens of penetrator and penetrated. You can play with the givens, even deny them: you're still acknowledging them. The individual can play with the general, but never escapes it: sex is not about treating individuals as ends in themselves. It isn't fair. Kant is the primary example of such liberal disapproval on the grounds that sex isn't fair.[71] Feminist thought agrees.[72]

6.934 The physical qualities men admire in other men are not necessarily those that women admire. "Bar muscles" are generally low on women's list of things they admire in men. "Curls for girls" is nonsense.

6.9341 Men are more interested in each others' muscles than, typically, women are. Men admire muscle as a sign of other men's masculinity and power. In someone they can merely admire, they admire. In someone they must fight, they counter.

Men can simply admire the contestants in a body-building contest. Contestants are there for the viewers to look at. They don't admire a man with whom they have to compete themselves.

Because all men are potential competitors, they will rarely compliment another man on what he looks like.

6.935 Men's initial point of departure with other men is hostility. Men see other men as threats, unless the situation allows them to feel that the other men are not threats. Men are magnets whose like poles repel each other.

For this reason they are capable of passionate attachment to other men when the polarities are reversed. This is called male bonding. It is so intense because it washes in on a flood of relief that the other men are there to help them, not attack them.

6.936 Men spend their lives in a constant low-level state of siege with respect to most other men. Men are always on their guard, at least initially.

For this reason most men place such value on knowing by sight who is where on the power scale. Most men want to be able to look at another person and know immediately, Do I have to oppose this person (male)? Or do I have the upper hand (female)? Must I be tensed (male) or relaxed (female)?

6.9361 Male bonding is homoerotic, but it is also quite chaste: no touching below the shoulders, or except in crashing into the other men.

6.94 Male hostility to other men is not because of women

6.95 Female hostility to other women is, to a much greater degree, because of men.

6.951 Sexual relations are asymmetrical. It matters whether a person is born male or female. This is not determinative, but the difference matters. It creates givens the individual must acknowledge, even if s/he departs from them.

6.96 Men typically despise the beings they vanquish. Being a sexual "top" is in a sense vanquishing another human being. The result is, men are naturally misogynistic with respect to the women who are their bottoms.

Straight sexuality is marked by a broad streak of misogyny.

6.961 Women who bottom are more acceptable than men who bottom. Men assume that women must be penetrated: that is their biological role. They may love the women they penetrate, and in any case the woman can't help being penetrated. This gives men another reason to despise women.

6.97 Men are constantly testing each other to make sure that they are not assuming a subordinate position with respect to another man, even a non-sexual one.

6.971 The mixture of desire to penetrate women, the feeling that after all women can't help being the ones penetrated, and protection of a subservient creature that a man has uses for create the feelings towards women we call "courtly." Men can allow themselves to "let go" with women in a way they cannot with men. Women are men's institutionalized weaknesses. A man may say to his buddies, with no apology, "I'm whipped" (a short form of "pussy-whipped"), meaning that he will do anything his woman says. He will not acknowledge this degree of subservience to other men.

Why do we argue and how do we win arguments?

7 Arguments between individuals or groups arise over the distinction each of us makes between project and unorganized territory. The sum total of all arguing positions is the world.

7.01 Arguments are always about whether or not the pathway includes certain things or whether it excludes them.

7.02 Arguments take the form of challenges to an unquestioned position, and the response, back and forth. All arguments presuppose placement of those arguing. The arguments make the placements clear.

7.03 Arguments are always over rubrics: what is included, what is excluded.

Arguments are attempts to change the world. Sometimes they succeed.

7.1 The attempt to convince people of something typically takes the form of saying that what they are dead set against doing is in fact the same as something they approve of. X is really Y, where Y is something the other person has already signed off on. The response to this argument will be, X isn't Y. Reasons given for why X is or isn't Y don't prove or disprove the contention, because either you accept that X is Y or you don't. All the reasons do is give a name to the distinction. They either erase the distinction between X and Y, or insist upon it.

7.12 If I let my daughter approach the neighbors to sell Girl Scout cookies, but don't want others doing that to me, I have to explain why the neighbors and I are not one category, but two. Or perhaps the distinction lies between the girls. Their daughter is a loud-mouthed bully. Or perhaps my situation is what is different: I have a baby who will be woken up. Or: I can't eat candy because I am a diabetic. And so on.

7.121 When I give up arguing and let the neighbor's daughter try to sell me Girl Scout cookies, it is not because the words for the argument are lacking. It is because I don't see any reason to invoke them. Maybe I agree that there is no reason why my daughter should be treated differently, or the neighbor counters that he too has a child that may be awoken. We say this is "being convinced."

Arguments are like an infinite board game: all the squares exist in advance. The only thing that varies is whether and how we fill them.

If we look at the pattern of words as if from Mt. Olympus, we see an infinite number of steps that have simply not been taken by the individual, for whatever reason.

7.13 Take the assertion that something isn't "natural." But it occurs in nature, comes the answer. Maybe, comes the response, but it doesn't result in X. Does this mean that any act that doesn't result in X is unnatural? says the challenger. This is at least three moves for each piece on the board.

The person arguing need not give in at this point if s/he is set against doing so. All s/he need do is say, there *is* a distinction between these two things. Ideally, the person gives a name to this distinction, which may be called distinction-currently-without-a-name, and is home free, theoretically speaking. (The other person may not be convinced.) Or someone else more adept at words names it.

7.14 Kant identified something without a name that he needed for his argument, and gave it a name. It had to be something that was neither true by definition nor a fact in the world, a judgment of taste more true than the expression of an individual's likes or dislikes. He identified the space, the "synthetic a priori."[73] He could just as well have called it the not-A, not-B, or the whatsit. (Perhaps, in German, das Wie-dem-auch-sei.)

7.15 Etiquette is largely based on publicly acknowledging the same rubrics as other people. That is to say, the same distinctions.

We say "sir" to a superior to show that we see things the same way he does, that we are in a subordinate position. A "presumptuous" tone of voice is inappropriate under certain circumstances, because it suggests we do not understand how things stand. So is an angry tone of voice inappropriate. Or a hectoring one.

7.151 In *Anna Karenina* Vronsky goes to visit his horse groom before the big race in which he falls and Anna betrays her love for him.[74] He is also serving as his own jockey. His groom asks him where he is going. Vronsky is initially offended: grooms do not ask aristocratic owners where they are going. But he realizes after a moment's reflection that the groom is asking not the master, but the jockey. Grooms need to know that jockeys will be close by. Vronsky is immediately calmed. The question fits with a certain order, where he fits in the category of "jockey" (but not of aristocrat), and so is appropriate.

7.16 Arguments fail to happen if people retreat into belief as weapons: I believe X; say what you will.

7.2 Using words is an action. There was in each case a time when they were not. Words surge from silence.

The person who uses words, whether oral or written, ruptures the default of silence because s/he feels that the world is out of joint. Others may not feel that way.

Arguments are always attempts to change the world. Sometimes they succeed.

7.21 What causes authors to write works? We can say after the works exist, but not before, precisely because the works don't exist. Works made of words come from a nowhere that can be mapped only subsequently.

7.22 Questions are not waiting to be asked. We have to ask them. To the person who asks this question, it had to be asked. To almost all others, it comes as quite a surprise.

The person asking the question regarded things as they are with amazement. (See 4.791.)

7.23 The world is full of questions, actual, possible, abandoned. Most are never asked, and at any given time only one is on the table.

7.231 Not asking this question is not a sign of stupidity. It is merely a sign of not being the person who asks it, not being placed where s/he is, or perhaps being so placed but lacking the will or need to challenge the world.

Typically, the most grateful supporters of someone who asks this question will be someone of this last sort, someone placed in the same spot but unwilling or unable to articulate it.

Home-field advantage

7.24 Arguments are typically attacks on unquestioned positions. The unquestioned argument has the "home-field" advantage.

7.241 The failure of someone with the home-field advantage to question the position s/he holds is merely the nature of someone doing what s/he does.

7.242 The challenger, however, needs to imply that the person with the home-field advantage should have questioned this position sooner, or never held it to begin with. But that is what the challenger is trying to accomplish. This may be the result of their actions. What sense does it make to say the world should have been such as to make this action unnecessary?

7.25 Arguments take place as alternatives to other things, such as battles, or hiring a hit man. They are a sign of restrictions on action in a social system.

7.251 Each side may fail to realize that in engaging in the project of arguing, they are failing to engage in a multitude of other projects.

7.252 Arguments are merely the inter-personal form of alteration. We can argue with ourselves. Instead we usually just change. Frequently we are not even aware that we have changed until someone else points it out to us.

7.253 The person with the home-field advantage has reached what game theory calls a saddle point with respect to his or her own projects.

The person in the challenger's position is the one who wants change.

7.26 If a question seems to us to demand asking, we ask it. We make an argument for our position. This means, we describe the world in a way that includes us. As currently described, the world excludes us.

7.261 Contemporary academic arguments influenced by Foucault feel sorry for those trying to change the world by pointing out that they have an uphill battle. Of course they do. This is the nature of trying to change the world. Those trying to keep their home-field advantage are merely playing the very game those challenging them are in turn asking to play, not keeping others out of the game.

7.262 Being in the game means carving a place for yourself.

7.27 Arguments are between descriptions of the world that either include the viewpoint of the person making the attack, or exclude it.

The argument we make is determined by where we are placed: are we on the offensive or the defensive?

7.271 A letter to the advice columnist Ann Landers gives an example. A woman writes in to say that she feels that dinner guests in her house should not get out of their seats to get condiments like ketchup. For her, the fundamental likeness of the situation is with a restaurant. In a restaurant, she reasons, people do not get out of their seats. Therefore they should not in her house either.

Ann acknowledges that in restaurants, people stay seated. She also accepts a single rubric for dinner at a house and dinner in a restaurant: both are dinners. But she makes a distinction at another level. She sees the sitting in the chair as less important than the project common to a restaurant and a private house of making sure people get what they want. In a restaurant, she says, this is accomplished one way, in a private house, another. Ergo, the person may get out of her seat.

7.2711 People may have determined that the issue will be decided by Ann. They do not see a resolution to their conflict, so this is the means they have agreed upon to solve their problem. They could just as well have agreed to flip a coin, or to trial by fire.

Resolution of arguments doesn't necessarily mean the arguments have accomplished anything besides making clear the differences of those arguing. It only means we agree to end them. Arguments never go away. In the same way, questions of philosophy are merely abandoned.

The twentieth century didn't solve the question of the nature of meaning. It simply beat the drum so long people got tired of listening. It defined a territory of how this group of people talked abut this subject.

We still don't know how many angels can dance on the head of a pin, or whether other people are real or not, or what unifies the self—all of which were once very important, pressing questions. Now they are merely historical. We've ceased to care. So we teach them in philosophy classes.

Apparently our lives can in fact go on without having answers to these questions.

7.2712 Believing that arguments must be solved by argument is like failing to understand that the Gordian knot can be cut—or simply walked away from.

7.28 If something cannot be resolved in argument, we must agree to end it some other way, if we are to stay within common parameters.

7.281 One day I looked up from the hammock in my back yard to realize that something was strange about the corner of the yard. It took a minute or two before I realized what it was: the brightly-colored plastic play set my daughter used to play on was gone, with its imprint still clearly in the grass. Also missing were the plastic play sets from the house whose yard adjoined mine, whose owners, with their little boy, had moved out weeks ago. I wondered if there was a connection.

I went over to talk to the new owners, but found only a neighbor who said they hadn't moved in yet. However the neighbor had seen workmen hauling away plastic play sets the week before. She thought I should contact the new owners by letter. I did so.

The result was an infuriated telephone call from the wife, who immediately acknowledged having had all plastic play sets hauled away. The ensuing argument revolved around the question, Was the more fundamental rubric that of large plastic play sets, which were to be hauled away, or did the fact that one of them was clearly on my property put it in another category? For my new neighbor, the more fundamental rubric was the first. All were plastic play sets, and all were to be hauled away.

I knew how the world at large would answer this question of whether my version was more believable or hers, so I could afford to be bemused at this. For everyone else besides this woman, what is mine is mine and what is hers is hers, even if the two things resemble each other. For her, the resemblance trumped ownership.

The matter was resolved by a policeman visiting my neighbor, at my suggestion. She gave in, though she made clear she was not convinced. In her mind, the most fundamental category was different than I knew most other people thought it was.

7.282 If she had not given in, the issue might have gone to court.

Litigation

7.283 Lawyers link the unknown to the known, to generally shared projects. The draw lines from a patch of unexplored ground off the pathway to the closest plausible pathway, saying: The unknown territory is closest to this bit of known territory, or that.

Two lawyers give competing versions of how to connect the unknown with the known. A judge or jury decides which is the more successful link.

In the case of the play set, the link was fairly obvious, to the distinction between my property and hers. No one but the woman would find her argument plausible, the one linking plastic play sets to plastic play sets. In other cases resolving a conflict is more difficult.

This doesn't mean she was wrong, only that hers was not the view generally accepted. I knew this was the case; apparently she didn't.

7.284 The more difficult the legal case, the more arbitrary the ultimate decision, which could have gone either way.

Having a judge decide one way or the other doesn't mean the people involved are convinced, only that they agree to end the argument. The court is the means agreed upon in such cases.

Kleist's Michael Kohlhaas, who ruined himself pursuing what he thought of as justice in a minor case, stands as an example of what happens to people who think they are going to get the world to mirror their own projects.[75]

7.3 Arguments ensue when other people's projects clash with our own.

7.31 Systems of ethics are attempts to avoid arguments.

7.32 Most of the world never enters into the collision that is implied in an argument, or a court case. Should I eat an ice cream cone or read John Stuart Mill? We probably don't understand why the question should be asked, but at least it makes sense. We can imagine someone having the reason to ask it.

A question that doesn't even seem to make sense is this: Bees or beeswax? Bees or beeswax *what?* we would say. In what way are these alternatives? What are the issues here? We can't answer these questions till we know what the project is. What is the goal? Is the goal satisfaction of hunger or mental stimulation?

7.33 Because written works stay around past the death of their immediate contexts, sometimes we are hard-pressed to understand what questions they are trying to resolve.

When we read a new work, we would do well to ask, What is the question they are trying to answer? If we don't see what this is, we can't understand the work.

7.4 Most of the questions in the world are never asked. Most of the world is never charted by the tenets of ethics, which delineate projects.

Most of the world is off to the side of our projects. Conflict always presupposes the project. What is off to the side doesn't conflict with anything.

7.41 We can make a link of any given point to the high road, but we have to have a reason to do so. And that is still the link of only one point to the high road, not of the point next to it, or one far away on the other side.

The link isn't necessarily ideal. It may be merely the best link we can make under the circumstances. But if we agree to accept this, it becomes the link of record.

7.42 Professional talkers and thinkers—academics in particular—like to conceive the world as being full of collisions. The worldview they teach is one of linked issues: Romanticism is a reaction to Classicism. Kant is responding to Hume. Modernism is both like, and unlike, Romanticism.

This is a Hollywood movie version of the world, all full of drama and car crashes: there's something going on every minute.

But this is not the nature of the world. Most things float in the void and never touch each other, never conflict. They are all on the vast open spaces of the uncharted world. Zephyrs don't touch John Stuart Mill. The works of a sixteenth century poet doesn't touch the railing of my deck. All are in the world.

7.5 Arguments need not change people's minds.

7.501 Arguments need never end. There is always an answer to the answer we have heard.

The next space is always already plotted on the board game. Only we can decide if we wish to move to it. If we do, the argument continues.

7.502 Nonetheless we usually do stop arguing. Sometimes we even change our minds. We say we have been convinced. All this means is: we decide to abandon the argument.

7.503 Someone looking on from above sees us turn around on the road. They say, "I guess he changed his mind." Or: "I guess he forgot something." They don't explain why the change of mind happened just then, or why just then we realized we forgot something.

7.5031 Some readers of the later Wittgenstein, author of the *Philosophical Investigations*, have thought his point was that changing our mind could only mean what was visible from the outside. That there was nothing else.

7.5032 In fact Wittgenstein's point was that whatever happens in the world, only something that doesn't exist yet—an explanation yet to be made—can explain this. It's not what is in the world that allows it to go forward, but what isn't—yet.

It's this "not yet articulated" that allows the change to happen. "Not yet articulated" can also mean, never articulated. We don't have the explanation (yet). We may never have it. And yet the thing has happened.

That is the way explanation works. (See 5.32.)

7.504 Things are happening all the time for which we don't ask for explanations. Something more fundamental than either the before state or the after state allowed the change to come to be.

We're unaware of this layer, even in absent form, until the change happens. Then we can postulate it. This is prior to articulating it.

7.51 It may not be the argument that has caused the change of mind. We may not ever be able to say what has caused the change of mind.

7.511 A glass may shatter at a single tap. But in order for this to happen it almost had to have been weakened invisibly by other things before.

We can always look for an explanation of the weakening. We need never find it.

7.52 Words determine our worlds to the extent that they become part of the projects. If part of our project is saying, "life begins at conception," saying this becomes an end in itself. We defend these words, and try to make others say them.

We can take anything as a project. If our project is to defend the installation of a huge piece of stone bearing the Ten Commandments in a public place on the grounds that this honors God, then that is our project. We don't listen to others who have other ways to "honor God" or who question the necessity of the project at all. For us, the world is binary. Any alternative action is dishonoring God.

All credos are made part of the project. All organized religion becomes part of the project.

7.53 If my point of departure is that life is a testing ground for how I will spend eternity, I will have one set of projects. If I tell myself that life is given to me to be enjoyed, I will have another. At any time we are engaged in our projects, we fail to question the direction of the projects. We fail to question the story, to disagree with ourselves.

7.531 Such a story about what happens beyond our field of perception must always be correctly placed with respect to what we know and what can be verified. It must be placed beyond this point.

No one can argue us out of a story, such as that this and so happens when we die, if it is correctly placed. That is the nature of its placement. Nothing proves it, to be sure, but nothing disproves it either.

7.54 The more fundamental the project and the story that justifies it, the less likely I'll be to alter it. It's just too difficult to do and requires re-arranging too many things. A mere argument with someone else whose projects are different probably isn't going to change much. It usually takes event on the order of magnitude of the death of a loved one to change us.

7.5401 Realizing that, when we talk to other people, we are dealing with complex creatures that are not necessarily going to change to our point of view is part of the humility needed for living.

We presuppose our own contexts and can be at the moment where we are. Thus we can focus only on the direction we're moving in.

When we talk to another person we have to deal with the whole line, not just action into the future.

7.5402 Intellectuals are particularly prone to forgetting they are dealing with people, not with walking ideas.

Of course the next response is there in embryo, in theory. We may forget that it's always there, and we always at some point fail to make it, cause it to become actual. So why should we be upset that the other person is failing to actualize this one, right here?

Someone may reject what we say because of the way we say it. This is not being irrational, it's just focusing on something we hadn't thought they'd focus on, or hadn't wanted them to.

7.541 But an argument *might* change us, or our argument someone else. At least it might be the thin edge of the wedge. We might alter our lives years after an argument with someone who grew red in the face and thought s/he had failed to influence us.

Still, we never know which aspect of an encounter it was that was decisive, even if the person "changes his mind." Was it our words? Our means of delivery? The timing? The other person being suddenly sick of the person trying to convince them of the opposite? Arguers typically always take credit for alterations there's no evidence they effected.

7.542 Like books that we read without comprehension at 20 and find riveting at 40, arguments can work like time bombs. Because they arise from places off our project grid, we don't know how they will affect us.

At the time we would have said they had no effect on us. Later we say they did.

7.55 What is the value of any change of mind? Why need others be like us? Does this make our position more right?

Certainty

7.6 We spend our lives in the attempt to pin things down, make the world certain. In the moment of pinning down, it feels as if we have achieved our goal. But we have only pinned down one thing, the thing we are considering right here, right now.

This is the nature of certainty. We might say we are now certain about the nature of certainty. But if this is so, nothing is changed. If it's true, this has always been the nature of certainty, even when we thought it wasn't. And it didn't bother us then. Somehow we continued to function anyway.

7.601. We might say: being certain really means: "This thing is certain until and unless it isn't"?

But we say it by saying: "It's certain" or "I'm certain." It means, I see no way to untie the Gordian knot. Or: it cannot be untied.

7.602 Perhaps we can say we're sure because nothing that could happen to the knot (such as cutting) counts as "untying." Give me whatever solution you will, I won't accept it.

But is this a statement about me, or about the knot?

Can we tell the difference?

7.61 Because we are linear creatures, considering first one thing, then another, then another, all we have pinned down is this right here, right now.

7.62 This is so even if what we have pinned down involves an assertion about the future.

So perhaps we have pinned down the future.

7.63 We can offer an image of the whole world, such as a river, or a pyramid, or a vale of tears. We mean this to apply to points further down the river, or elsewhere on the pyramid, or for the rest of the vale. In that sense we control the future. We want to include things we haven't thought of yet.

All we have included are things we have thought of, even if one of those is a reference to things we haven't thought of.

7.64 The attempt to articulate principles more fundamental than others is the attempt to protect ourselves against Burnham Wood coming to Dunsinane. As a result, we know that this thing will never happen. Unless it does, in which case we can look to explain it (the scientific point of view) or take it as a miracle. In neither case have we prevented it from happening.

7.641 Taking it as a miracle means we say that it transcends explanation: that's the meaning of this explanation that it's a miracle.

Nonetheless someone may explain it.

7.642 The distinction between form and content is an attempt to protect ourselves against the future. We domesticate change by relegating it to a lower level that we need not be concerned with. This is content. We assert that the form never changes.

Delineating Fundamental Ideas and Structures are the attempt to protect ourselves against the future.

7.643 We may say that all thought, whatever its content, is thus and so. (This was Kant's attempt to domesticate change). All such theories make the changes subordinate to the consistency.

But why should the thing subordinated accept this position?

7.65 All distinctions presuppose a cardinal ordering. We argue about whether A is on top of B, or B on top of A. Yertle wants to be on top of it all.

7.66 Yet most of the world isn't ordered with respect to either A or B, whatever these are. The molecular structure of iron may be more fundamental than any piece of iron, but what relationship does it have to a sense of humor? The west wind? The GNP of Bermuda? What have zephyrs to do with John Stuart Mill?

7.661 The belief that the world is intrinsically linked together is only justified when we look at things that are linked.

Most people like the security of looking at linked things and so rarely look elsewhere.

Predicting the future

7.7 Because we are unaware of our presuppositions until they are questioned, all we can be aware of are the presuppositions we are aware of. Not being aware of something doesn't mean it doesn't exist. Not predicting something in the future doesn't mean it isn't going to happen.

7.71 We all put things under rubrics without articulating these rubrics. Macbeth didn't articulate the principle that cut-off branches didn't figure under the rubric "woods."

7.712 Science attempts to use language not in common use and so without the multiple contexts that make such misunderstandings possible. A term has been invented to have a precise meaning. It seems we can have certainty with those things.

7.72 An invented word seems to make pinning down the future easier, as the attempt of logical positivists like Carnap, inspired by his reading of the *Tractatus*, to produce a cleansed version of language where arguments were impossible, makes agreement possible.[76] It's just that the more cleaned up the language and so the more absolutely it lends itself to statements no one is going to argue about, the less use it seems to be.

7.721 This is Wittgenstein's point with respect to logic, and mathematics, in the *Tractatus*. The more certain they are, the less information they give us about anything but themselves.

7.73 Purified language can produce statements that are more argument-proof than others. But the only way to produce statements that will never be abandoned is to say that by definition they are statements that deflect all objections.

But what if someone comes along and objects to the notion of statements that deflect all objections? Or simply walks away? Either way the argument loses its power. Even this cannot be assured to control the future.

7.731 This means that they fail to achieve their goal, which is to give us certainty about the future.

7.732 Mathematics is not a separate realm, it is merely a kind of language invented so as to be free of the reek of the human. Because humans have invented it, this is only a relative quality: its freedom is with respect to our lack of freedom. And we were the ones who invented it.

$2 + 2$ may always $= 4$, but we sense that this doesn't give us knowledge.

In the same way, Keats's urn is only different from life by dint of one specific comparison (the nature of the love depicted on it vs. Earthly love). In some ways it *is* life: it is a piece of stone, and so can be broken as easily as the people the poet says it outlives.

7.733 It should come as no surprise that we constantly find aspects of mathematics that are quite human indeed.

This is so for the same reason that science is shown to have reached conclusions we now reject.

Mathematics is merely the language that transcends: because it borders on the normal language it constantly has to give up pieces of its territory and move outward.

7.8 Words that claim validity for more than their place in the line of 1 + 1 + 1 + 1 that is human thought use vector arrows that gesture towards the future. Still, that is merely the nature of these words. It does not change the fact that all together they constitute only a single 1 that will be succeeded by the following 1. Each new generation is new.

Such words, say an image of all of life, or a fundamental distinction between form and content, are like a sign on one person's suburban lot with an arrow over to the other, like Yertle, saying: I include the other lot too.

The other lot may not agree. It probably doesn't even know the claim has been made.

In any case the reference is only to the next lot. It doesn't take account of all the rest of the uncharted world, that which falls off the paths of the projects.

7.9 Wittgenstein's attempt, in the *Tractatus,* was to solve all problems once and for all so we didn't have to argue.

He wanted to control the future utterly. This is why he was sure to fail. The *Tractatus* was a work set up to go up in smoke; the point was the explosion.

Controlling the world

7.901 All conceptualizations, all arguments, are the form that our humanity takes within a system that discourages other actions.

7.902 Clausewitz said, "war is politics by other means."[77] He may have meant that with respect to talking, action leading to death was appealing to a higher level. It was a way of ending argument.

7.903 Clausewitz also wrote movingly of what he called the "fog of war," the fact that in a clash, the best-laid plans go quickly agley. You can go into battle saying that A, B, and C will happen, but things are very likely to derail at A, or even before.

7.904 Strategists always cite the "ironclad" Schlieffen plan of the Germans to take Paris in World War I as a warning against too-great hubris in battle. You can move toy soldiers around on a table, but that's the only time you get to determine the outcome of a battle.

7.91 All ideas are finite. All conceptualizations are finite. This means, they can be put aside.

7.92 Many people try to control the physical world after our deaths. We write wills obliging people to do this and so. We set up headstones of the hardest materials we know, little thinking that these too can be eroded, or fall victim to vandals. We fail to consider that the land in which our remains are set may one day be put to other uses, or be washed away by rising seas.

We may dream of an afterlife that allows us none of the qualities that made us who we are. The more certain it seems, the more removed from anything we can imagine. Does my after-spirit like chardonnay? Is it male? Is it young and potent, or old an impotent, or non-sexual? But if it is non-everything that made me, at various times, me, what sense does it make to say it's *my* afterlife-spirit? Does it even remember having been alive?

7.93 The relationship between the degree of dissemination of that part of us that achieves Earthly immortality and how true to life it is is an inverse one. Marilyn Monroe for most people is the woman with her dress being blown up, a single moment in a single film. (See 4.822.) We remember this image precisely because it fails to do justice to the reality of the woman. It's a single image asked to stand in for a whole life: cups of coffee, restless nights, a smell here, a face there. All of it rolled into a woman with her skirt up.

The stronger the immortality is, the less it really immortalizes the person.

7.931 People will by definition make personal versions of what is widely disseminated. This is the revenge of the personal on the general. Rock may break scissors, but paper wraps rock.

For me, Abraham Lincoln is a smear of glue. When I was in the first grade, I had chicken pox. During my absence, the other first graders had cut out pictures of Abraham Lincoln and glued them onto pieces of paper. The teacher had made one for me. When the pictures dried, they revealed the smears of mucilage underneath. She brought it to me. I looked at it for hours on end. I can still see Abraham Lincoln as a boy in the picture. Underneath is mucilage.

7.9311 Growing up, as Proust learned, means trading these personal associations for the less interesting general things adults know. Abraham Lincoln became the President who issued the Emancipation Proclamation, and so on. I no longer speak about the smear of mucilage when I speak of Abraham Lincoln, knowing that each person has his or her own associations we agree not to talk about in public.

7.9312 Even so, the few facts I can scrape together about Lincoln before I trail off into the realm of my ignorance seem as far from the real man as the picture of Marilyn Monroe with her skirt up from the real woman.

7.932 The more of my life I dedicate to learning about someone, the closer to that person I may come. But this too is an inverse: the further I become from others.

If I spend my time becoming the custodian of only one person's immortality, I know a person no one else knows.

7.933 Our immortality is in any case limited by the fact that our successors may well tire of doing nothing but tending our altars.

At some point the living will rebel against the duties to the dead that prevent them from living, or devolve the responsibility off onto priests, libraries, or the Internet. We give up the attempt to hold everything before our eyes, and accept our limitation in the larger scheme of things.

Death and ageing

7.94 The death of each moment in the next is no less absolute than the death of a person.

The displacement of one idea in our minds by another is no less complete.

7.941 It only seems tragic to think that the young grow jowly and then wither when we consider this from the outside, seeing the person's projects silhouetted against the rest of the world.

To the person locked inside this body and these projects, the situation isn't tragic, any more than our own lives are to ourselves. We are like apples that grow large and plump to serve seeds of action. When the seeds mature, the flesh wrinkles and then dissolves. It was created to serve only these seeds.

We use up our bodies in our projects. We are logs consumed by the fire of life, as Shakespeare suggested in Sonnet 73.

7.942 Sometimes when we look in the mirror we are startled: who is this old man or old woman? We frequently say, we are the same person inside, unchanged. This doesn't necessarily mean that in fact we are unified beings that don't change. We're saying that we are not in that moment processing one of the millions of changes that we must process daily.

What we see is the change.

7.943 We can focus on the changes that make us many people, or the threads that continue.

Neither predominates intrinsically.

7.944 Why do we think we have to articulate the world in order for it to be?

7.95 We define our place in the world, we do not define the world.

We can articulate only the things that define us. Whatever we articulate defines us.

7.951 Our solutions are specific solutions, to specific problems. We have no guarantee that others will have these problems, or need these solutions.

7.952 These words, these arguments, these images, are like a ladder that gets us to another spot. We may then kick the ladder away. We don't need it any more.

At this point others come along and find the ladder we have kicked away. They say, this is useful.

7.9521 There are no implications for others, or for ourselves later, in the fact that we have found this ladder useless right here, right now.

We can even put the ladder in the Closet for Useless Ladders and lock the door. Yet if we try to do this, someone will always unlock it later on, or break the door down.

7.96 Talk is part of negotiating the difficulties we encounter in defining and carrying out our projects.

7.961 Others may find this talk, frozen into written works, useful in part or in whole in solving their own problems. Then again, they may not.

Talking ourselves silent

7.97 Anything there is can be talked about.

7.972 The only thing we can't do is talk our way beneath the endless skittering across the surface of our words. All words are only other words, even if what they say is, "I am not like other words."

We can never talk ourselves silent, except temporarily.

Any attempt to articulate The Problem will by definition only be the articulation of yet another problem.

7.98 Of course, we can stop talking. But we can always start again.

7.99 No one of us, or finite number, is the world. But we are parts of the world.

Our life includes our attempts to conceptualize it in talk.

We exhibit our role as parts of the whole, no matter what we do.

Whatever we do becomes our role.

Talking is part of our role. Even denying all of this is part of our role, something we can do. So too is being ignorant of all this.

7.991 Insofar as we are parts of the whole, we are limitless. Insofar as we are only parts, we are quite limited indeed. We are both of these simultaneously.

7.992 All that we do as individuals to transcend our individuality only expresses it more absolutely.

7.9921 Trying to sum up the world or stop it in its tracks is itself one thing we can do as creatures of motion. This doesn't mean we shouldn't do this, only that something links this stop with the motions around us that's more fundamental than either. We can ultimately articulate this thing, but that too is part of the motion of the world. And then what allows us to stop the world in articulation at that level recedes a level further down, where it in turn is amenable to articulation some day if people wish to articulate it.

7.9922 They can very well not want to articulate it, in which case it isn't articulated and is as if it did not exist.

What existed before the articulation isn't zero, but it isn't anything either. It's what we call "life," the thing that makes any particular thing possible.

7.993 Realizing this is the source of a sense of the mystical, the holy.

7.994 Because only those who are weary of talk come to the place of the holy, those who find this place are likely to say: —This is the place of things that cannot be said. And concerning what cannot be said, we must fall silent.

7.995 In fact, they should say, —Anything can be said. We can even talk of what cannot be said.

But realizing this may rob us of the desire to say it. If it does, we fall silent.

7.9951 The desire to talk may come back.

Endnotes

[1] Karl Marx and Sigmund Freud. In numerous texts, as a basic pattern of their thought structures.

[2] Theodore Seuss Geisel (pseud. Dr. Seuss), *Yertle the Turtle and Other Stories.*

[3] *New York Review of Books*, ed. Robert Silver, 1755 Broadway, New York, New York 10019.

[4] Ernest Hemingway, *A Moveable Feast.*

[5] In "Identity: A play," in Ulla Dydo, editor, *A Gertrude Stein Reader*, 588-594.

[6] Virginia Woolf, "The Mark on the Wall," in *The Complete Shorter Fiction of Virginia Woolf.*

[7] Count Leo Tolstoy, "The Kreutzer Sonata."

[8] George Lakoff and Mark Johnson, in *Metaphors We Live By.* The authors seem to believe that virtually all articulations are some degree metaphors. This isn't true. If we say an idea is "old" is this metaphoric or literal? We can't say whether we're thinking of old people and applying this to ideas, or whether an idea can, in a non-metaphoric way, be old. If we say someone draws a "sharp" distinction, is this metaphoric? It seems to be, as it evokes knives. But how about a "precise" distinction? Can a distinction be anything aside from a one of a set of adjectives invented for itself? How about the phrase "aside from" in the previous sentence: is this metaphoric (put to one side)? Or is this just what we say? Is it metaphoric or literal to speak of a "curfew"? It is a corruption of the French "couvre-feu," the hour when the fires were covered. But not even French speakers think of covering fires. This seems an example of what the poet Shelley, in his "Defense of Poetry," called a "dead metaphor." But these are quite rare, when we can see the old usage under the current one as a palimpsest. How about when we say that love is a thing we're all striving to attain. Is love a thing? If not, what is it? A feeling? A state of being? We can't even say. Can we "attain" love in a literal sense? Or is this a metaphor for tangible goals we can attain? In fact metaphors are only one possibility for relating worlds in a world with many possibilities; words are connected in a net of associations so thick it doesn't make sense to conceive of "metaphors" as any sort of explanatory concept somehow more primary than all the other possibilities.

[9] T.S. Eliot, "East Coker," from the "Four Quartets" (26).

[10] Franz Kafka, "Before the Law," in *The Metamorphosis, In the Penal Colony, and Other Stories*, 148-149.

[11] Robert Frost, "The Road Not Taken."

[12] John Keats, "Ode on a Grecian Urn."

[13] Michel Foucault, in such works as *Madness and Civilization*, *The Order of Things*, and *The Birth of the Clinic.*

[14] Malcolm Gladwell, *The Tipping Point: How Little Things Can Make a Big Difference.*

[15] Discussed in many places including Hans Abbing, *Why Artists are Poor: The Exceptional Economy of the Arts*, 107.

[16] Seven Harry Potter books are written by J.K. Rowlings and published by Scholastic.

[17] Thomas Wolfe, *You Can't Go Home Again.*

[18] George Orwell, *Burmese Days.* "Shooting an Elephant" is widely anthologized, as for example in *A Collection of Essays by George Orwell*, 154-161.

[19] Marcel Proust, *In Search of Lost Time.*

[20] William Wordsworth "Ode: Intimations of Immortality."

[21] René Magritte. For example "The Human Condition."

[22] *Ex Africa semper aliquid novi*—Pliny the Elder's note that Africa was always good for a surprise: "there's always something new coming from Africa."

[23] Jean-Paul Sartre, *Being and Nothingness.*

[24] Sigmund Freud, developed in numerous writings, as for example *The Interpretation of Dreams* (1924).

[25] Sartre, *Being and Nothingness.* Descartes, *Meditations.*

[26] *The Hours*, 2002, is based on a novel of the same name by Michael Cunningham. Both novel and movie contain Virginia Woolf as a character in a book whose title is one of her abandoned titles and to a degree imitates her style.

[27] Ruggero Leoncavallo, *I Pagliacci.*

[28] Immanuel Kant, *Critique of Judgment.*

[29] Brian de Palma, *Dressed to Kill*, 1980.

[30] William Makepeace Thackeray, *Vanity Fair.*

[31] Giacomo Puccini, *Tosca.*

[32] Aristotle, *Poetics.*

[33] Plato, *The Republic.* Plato famously denied poets a place in his ideal republic on the grounds that they produced "shadows of shadows," and so went further from Truth and the Ideal than even reality. John Searle, "The Logical Status of Fictional Discourse."

[34] Marcel Duchamps's urinal was entitled "Fountain" (1917).

[35] Victor Shklovsky, "Art as Technique."

[36] "Art makes the stone stoney," in "Art as Technique."

[37] John Searle, *Speech Acts: An Essay in the Philosophy of Language.*

[38] Emily Dickinson "There is no Frigate Like a Book," Complete Poems XCVI.

[39] Afred, Lord Tennyson, "Ulysses."

[40] Descartes, *Meditations,*

[41] Gilbert Ryle, developed in *The Concept of Mind.*

[42] Molière, "Le Bourgeois Gentilhomme."

[43] William Hazlitt, "On Genius and Common Sense."

[44] John Keats, "Ode on a Grecian Urn."

[45] Karl Marx and Friedrich Engels, "The Communist Manifesto."

[46] E. B. White, *Charlotte's Web.*

[47] As for example A. J. Ayer, *Language, Truth and Logic.*

[48] Descartes, *Meditations.*

[49] William Shakespeare, *Macbeth.*

[50] Sir Arthur Conan Doyle, "Silver Blaze."

[51] John Locke, *An Essay Concerning Human Understanding.*

[52] As explained in *Aztecs*, 33-34.

[53] Immanuel Kant, *Critique of Pure Reason.*

[54] Peirce, "Man's Glassy Essence."

[55] David Hume, *An Enquiry Concerning Human Understanding.* Karl Popper, *The Logic of Scientific Discovery.*

[56] Voltaire, *Candide or Optimism.*

[57] Karl Popper, *The Logic of Scientific Discovery.*

[58] Ludwig Wittgenstein, *Tractatus Logico-Philosophicus.*

[59] Robert Nozick, *Invariances.*

[60] Jean-Jacques Rousseau, *The Social Contract.* John Rawls, *A Theory of Justice.*

[61] Alexander Hamilton, John Jay, and James Madison, *The Federalist Papers.*

[62] Sigmund Freud, *Civilization and its Discontents.*

[63] Gustave Flaubert, *Madame Bovary.*

[64] An excellent selection of basic texts is in *Philosophy and Sex*, 3rd ed.

[65] St. Paul, in the Epistle to the Ephesians 5:22.

[66] Geza Vermes, *Jesus the Jew: A Historian's Reading of the Gospels.*

[67] *Candide*, Chapter 1.

[68] The unitive function of sex is treated in Pope Paul VI's encyclical, *Humanae Vitae.*

[69] For example, in Eve Sedgwick, *Between Men: English Literature and Male Homosexual Desire.*

[70] Michel Foucault, *The History of Sexuality: An Introduction.*

[71] In *Lectures on Ethics.*

[72] As in Andrea Dworkin, *Intercourse.*

[73] Kant, *Critique of Pure Reason.*

[74] Leo Tolstoy, *Anna Karenina* (Part II, Chapter XXI).

[75] Heinrich von Kleist, *Michael Kohlhaas.*

[76] Rudolf Carnap, *The Logical Structure of the World and Pseudoproblems in Philosophy.*

[77] Carl von Clausewitz, *On War.*

Bibliography

Abbing, Hans. *Why Artists are Poor: The Exceptional Economy of the Arts.* Amsterdam: Amsterdam University Press, 2004.

Aristotle, *Poetics.* New York: Penguin, 1996.

Ayer, A. J. *Language, Truth and Logic.* New York: Dover, 1952.

Baker, Robert B, Kathleen J. Winninger, and Frederick A. Elliston, eds. *Philosophy and Sex.* 3rd ed. Amherst, NY: Prometheus Books, 1998.

Carnap, Rudolf. *The Logical Structure of the World and Pseudoproblems in Philosophy.* Berkeley: University of California Press, 1983.

Clausewitz, Carl von. *On War.* New York: Everyman, 1993.

Corvino, John, ed. *Same Sex: Debating the Science, Ethics, and Culture of Homosexuality.* Lanham, MD: Rowman and Littlefield, 1997.

Doyle, Sir Arthur Conan. "Silver Blaze." In *Sherlock Holmes: Selected Stories*, 1-33. Oxford: Oxford University Press, 1998.

Dworkin, Andrea. *Intercourse.* New York: Basic Books, 2006.

Geisel, Theodore Seuss, pseud. Dr. Seuss. *Yertle the Turtle and Other Stories.* New York: Random House, 1986.

Eliot, T.S. "East Coker," 23-34. *Four Quartets.* New York: Harvest, 1968.

Foucault, Michel. *The Birth of the Clinic: An Archaeology of Medical Perception.* New York: Vintage, 1994.

---. *The History of Sexuality: An Introduction.* New York: Vintage, 1990.

---. *Madness and Civilization: A History of Insanity in the Age of Reason.* New York: Vintage, 1988.

---.*The Order of Things: An Archaeology of the Human Sciences.* New York: Vintage, 1994.

Frost, Robert, "The Road Not Taken." In *The Road Not Taken: A Selection of Robert Frost's Poems*, 220-271. New York: Owl, 2002.

Freud, Sigmund. *The Interpretation of Dreams.* New York: Penguin 1992.

Freud, Sigmund. *Civilization and its Discontents.* New York: Norton, 2005.

Gladwell, Malcolm. *The Tipping Point: How Little Things Can Make a Big Difference.* Boston: Back Bay, 2002.

Hamilton, Alexander, John Jay, and James Madison, *The Federalist Papers.* New York: Signet, 2003.

Hazlitt, William. "On Genius and Common Sense." In *English Romantic Writers,* ed. David Perkins, 656-662. New York: Harcourt, Brace, and World. 1967.

Hemingway, Ernest, *A Moveable Feast.* New York: Vintage, 2000.

Hume, David. *An Enqiry Concerning Human Understanding.* New York: Oxford University Press, 1999.

Kafka, Franz, "Before the Law." In *The Metamorphosis, In the Penal Colony, and Other Stories*, 148-149. New York: Schocken, 1995.

Kant, Immanuel. *Critique of the Power of Judgment*. Cambridge: Cambridge University Press, 2001.

---. *Critique of Pure Reason.* Cambridge: Cambridge University Press, 1999.

---. *Lectures on Ethics*. Edited by Peter Heath, J.B. Schneewind. Cambridge: Cambridge University Press, 2001.

Kleist, Heinrich von. *Michael Kohlhaas*. Stuttgart: Klett, 1993.

Lakoff, George and Mark Johnson. *Metaphors We Live By*. Chicago: University of Chicago Press, 2003.

Locke, John. *An Essay Concerning Human Understanding*. Amherst, NY: Prometheus, 1994.

Marx, Karl and Friedrich Engels. *The Communist Manifesto*. New York: Signet, 1998.

Moctezuma, Eduardo Matos and Felipe Solis Olguin. *Aztecs*. New York: Abrams, 2002.

Nozick, Robert. *Invariances: The Structure of the Objective World*. Cambrige: Harvard University Press, 2003.

Orwell, George. *Burmese Days*. New York: Harvest, 1974.

---."Shooting an Elephant." In *A Collection of Essays by George Orwell*, 154-161. New York: Doubleday, 1954.

Paul VI, Pope. "Humanae Vitae." In *Philosophy and Sex*, 3rd ed.. Edited by Robert B. Baker, Kathleen J. Winninger, and Frederick A. Elliston, 96-105. Amherst, NY: Prometheus Books, 1998.

Peirce, Charles S. "Man's Glassy Essence." In *Collected Papers of Charles Saunders Peirce, Vol VI.* Edited by Charles Hartshorne and Paul Weiss, 238-271. Cambridge, MA: Harvard University Press, 1935.

Popper, Karl. *The Logic of Scientific Discovery*. London: Routledge, 2002.

Plato, *The Republic*. New York: Penguin, 2003.

Proust, Marcel. *In Search of Lost Time* . Translated by C.K. Scott-Moncrieff, Terence Kilmartin and D. J. Enright. New York: Modern Library, 2003.

Rawls, John. *A Theory of Justice*. Cambridge: Harvard University Press, 2005.

Rousseau, Jean-Jacques. *The Social Contract. New York: Penguin, 1968.*

Ryle, Gilbert. *The Concept of Mind.* Chicago: University of Chicago Press, 2000.

Sartre, Jean-Paul. *Being and Nothingness*. New York: Washington Square, 1993.

Searle, John. "The Logical Status of Fictional Discourse." *New Literary History* 6 (1975): 319-32.

---. *Speech Acts: An Essay in the Philosophy of Language.* Cambridge: Cambridge University Press, 1970.

Sedgwick, Eve Kosovsky. *Between Men: English Literature and Male Homosexual Desire.* New York: Columbia University Press, 1986.

Shklovsky, Victor. "Art as Technique." In *Russian Formalist Criticism: Four Essays.* Edited by Lee T. Lemon and Marion Reis, 3-34. Lincoln, NE: University of Nebraska Press, 1965.

Stein, Gertrude. "Identity: A play." In Ulla Dydo, ed. *A Gertrude Stein Reader,* 588-594. Evanston, IL: Northwestern University Press, 1993.

Thackeray, William Makepeace. *Vanity Fair.* New York: Penguin, 2003.

Tolstoy, Count Leo. *Anna Karenina.* Translated by Constance Garnett. New York: Grosset and Dunlap, 1931.

---. *The Kreutzer Sonata and Other Stories.* Edited by David McDuff. New York: Penguin, 1986.

Vermes, Geza. *Jesus the Jew: A Historian's Reading of the Gospels.* Minneapolis: Augsburg Fortress, 1981.

Voltaire, *Candide or Optimism.* Edited by John Butt. New York: Penguin, 1950.

White, E.B. *Charlotte's Web.* New York: HarperCollins, 2001.

Wittgenstein, Ludwig. *Philosophical Investigations.* Upper Saddle River, NJ: Prentice-Hall, 1999.

---. *Tractatus Logico-Philosophicus.* New York: Routledge, 2001.

Wolfe, Thomas. *You Can't Go Home Again.* New York: Harper, 1998.

Woolf, Virginia. "The Mark on the Wall." In *The Complete Shorter Fiction of Virginia Woolf,* 2nd ed., 83-89. New York: Harvest, 1989.

Index

About the Author

Bruce Fleming is a professor of English at the U.S. Naval Academy, Annapolis. His most recent works include *Annapolis Autumn: Life, Death and Literature at the U.S. Naval Academy* (New Press, 2005) and *Why Liberals and Conservatives Clash* (Routledge, 2006). He has won an O. Henry award for short fiction and the Antioch Review Award for Distinctive Prose, a career award. Fleming is the author of a dozen books including the experimental novel *Twilley*, which critics compared to works by T.S. Eliot, Henry James, Proust, Thoreau, and David Lynch, and of a collection of dance essays called *Sex, Art and Audience*. His books for University Press of America include *Art and Argument, Science and the Self,* and *Sexual Ethics*, among others.

The author is a graduate of Haverford College, with subsequent degrees from the University of Chicago and Vanderbilt University. He studied in Paris and at the Universities of Munich and West Berlin, the last as a Fulbright Scholar. Before coming to Annapolis he taught at the University of Freiburg, West Germany, and, as a Fulbright Professor, at the National University of Rwanda.

www.ingramcontent.com/pod-product-compliance
Lightning Source LLC
Chambersburg PA
CBHW020356100426
42812CB00001B/87